T0271764

Stephen Joseph PhD, is a writer, psychotherapist and coaching psychologist. His previous books include *What Doesn't Kill Us: A Guide to Overcoming Adversity and Moving Forward* and *Authentic: How to be Yourself and Why it Matters*. His books have been translated into many languages and convey new and exciting psychological ideas in an accessible and helpful way.

Praise for *Think Like a Therapist*

'Illuminating, insightful, and a lovely read. Stephen Joseph has beautifully distilled the essence of psychotherapy to bring a book of wisdom and compassion with powerful lessons in living. Whether it is to untangle emotions or seek a new direction, this book will help you look at life afresh. It challenges us to ask ourselves the hard questions that we must answer if we are to learn to value ourselves, reclaim our personal power, and live a richer life. Anyone wanting a more balanced and happier life will benefit from this book'

Julia Samuel, psychotherapist, bestselling author and speaker

'Stephen Joseph has crafted the art of conveying complex concepts and ideas in an accessible way whilst maintaining the depth and rigour of the research and philosophical bases from which they are built. And he conveys these ideas in a kind, compassionate, and warm way that reflects him as a person. I would like to thank him for writing this book. *Think Like a Therapist* will enrich the process of self-development for anyone in a way that is made possible only by his depth and wealth of understanding the human condition. I will recommend it to students thinking about becoming therapists and to clients in therapy. Anyone thinking about therapy and self-development will learn a lot'

David Murphy, Professor of Psychology and Education at the University of Nottingham and editor of *Counselling Psychology: A Textbook for Study and Practice*

'This book is a rare gem – a masterclass in how to live a contented life – all told in Stephen's gentle caring voice. His six insights are irrefutably right: simple in meaning, yet very deep in truth. Anyone who actually follows what he offers, really will find it life-changing'

Richard Macklin, executive coach, The Alexander Partnership

'I love this book. The concept of sharing with people what an experienced therapist has learned about living life well is brilliant. The way Stephen Joseph mixes together his personal experience, clients' stories and research is a perfect balance. His writing is so conversational that people are going to feel like they are in a personal relationship'

Richard G. Tedeschi, Ph.D., Distinguished Chair, Boulder Crest Institute for Posttraumatic Growth

THINK LIKE
A THERAPIST

Six Life-Changing Insights for
Leading a Good Life

STEPHEN JOSEPH

PIATKUS

piatkus

First published in Great Britain in 2022 by Piatkus
This paperback edition published in 2023 by Piatkus

5 7 9 10 8 6 4

A CIP catalogue record for this book
is available from the British Library.

ISBN: 978-0-349-43187-1

Typeset in Miller Text by M Rules
Printed and bound in Great Britain by
Clays Ltd, Elcograf S.p.A.

Papers used by Piatkus are from well-managed forests
and other responsible sources.

Piatkus
An imprint of
Little, Brown Book Group
Carmelite House
50 Victoria Embankment
London EC4Y 0DZ

An Hachette UK Company
www.hachette.co.uk

www.littlebrown.co.uk

In memory of Colm Markey

Contents

Author's note

What is said in the therapy room is confidential so it is important to say that the stories in this book are a mixture of different people's experiences, with all personal details changed so that no one person is identifiable. In doing so, I have opted for an approach known as *faction*, where one tells a fictional story that incorporates real people and events. This provides what I think is the only ethical way to tell a fact-based story involving psychotherapy clients. Where a person is identifiable, they were not clients in therapy, they were interviewed specifically for the book and their consent was given.

It also seems important to explain that the term 'psychotherapy' means different things to different people. There are a range of approaches based on different ideas about what leads people to develop problems and how they can best be helped. My observations are not representative of all psychotherapists; these are my reflections, based on my personal experiences and professional learnings, about what matters and how I feel one can lead a good life.[1]

Prologue

A few years ago, I asked myself a question: if I could bottle the main lessons that I have learned as a psychotherapist, what would they be? On the surface, everything in my life was going well, but I was struggling inside. My motivation was low, I was finding it hard to make decisions and there wasn't much joy. Life is too short to live like this, I thought. A change of direction was called for. I needed to practise more of what I preached. After a lot of contemplation I came up with six fundamental truths that I think are the basis for a good life.

But what makes for a good life?

That is a question that has perplexed philosophers throughout the ages and is now posed by psychologists and psychotherapists like me. In essence a good life is a happy life, yet it is hard to pin down what people mean when they talk about happiness. It is not just one thing.

Happiness is about taking pleasure in life, but not so excessively that the pursuit of pleasure becomes all-important. It is about having a purpose in life and finding a sense of meaning, but not such that life itself is not lived. It is also about engaging in life in a way that is enriching and challenging such that we feel fulfilled, but not so much that we forget about other people. Happiness encompasses companionship, friendship and belonging, but not to such an extent that we lose ourselves. It involves understanding ourselves and knowing who we are, but not such that we become consumed only with thoughts of ourselves. All these things play a part.[1] The good life is in finding the right balance of each.

A tightrope walker can maintain their balance while walking along a tensioned wire using a long tool called a balancing pole and that is how I think of these six fundamental truths that I will describe – as providing us with lessons about how to live life wisely and keep our balance.

When I sat down to ask myself what the main lessons were, I was looking for a balancing pole for myself. Psychotherapists are like anyone else – sometimes things get out of balance – and so it was for me. Therapists have a training in well-being and mental health, but we are all human and not invulnerable. It is hard enough to walk a wire, as I remember from hours spent trying during my boyhood, but what makes it trickier to keep our balance is the unexpected and the uncontrollable breeze. The skill is to maintain balance despite the sway of the rope. In the same way, life throws up events that cause disturbances beyond our control.

As I said, before I began writing this book I was feeling unsettled. A lot had happened. In the space of five years, both my parents died from dreadful illnesses. That served as a forceful reminder that the same journey to the grave awaits me and all those I love and care about. It also brought home that a good life is one lived in the present, not postponed until tomorrow – which is what I felt I had been doing. I felt my life was trickling through my fingers like sand, that I was wasting each precious second. I wished I had spent more time with those close to me, done more things that brought happy memories to mind and created a richer life for myself and those around me. I felt weighed down with anxiety as I tried to manage the various demands in my life, but felt I was failing. I knew I had to regain my balance.

I also recognised that what I was experiencing wasn't much different from what many people go through. The future can often seem frightening. We try to create a sense of certainty in an uncertain world. We put off until tomorrow things that seem important while we manage what seems urgent today. Our friendships, interests, happiness and even our health can fall by the wayside, as we pursue our careers, try to find our place in the world and pay our bills. Life can be very difficult at times. With so many pressures on us, it is not surprising that many of us struggle to keep going.

The good life, though, is not just about how we are when all is going well in our lives. To lead a good life, we need to be able to navigate whatever is in front of us, to approach life as it is and not wait for tomorrow to start living. How we do that, how happy we are when things are not going well, and how much we can cope with adversity, depends on the perspective we take. And in trying to focus on what the most important lessons are for myself, I have managed to narrow them down to six areas. I hope that by sharing them with you in the chapters that follow, you will find something helpful too.

The last few years have been particularly difficult, as I have said, also given the various political crises, conflicts, wars and the pandemic, all of which have led to so much loss and suffering, along with the countless other challenges and stresses. When life throws unpleasant things at us that are hard to deal with, we need to keep our balance. If we don't, we can get lost in our emotions of worry, anger, irritation, guilt or shame and our attention and resources get so sucked up that we don't have time to stop and take stock of what's behind our emotions and what really matters to us.

The words and metaphors we use to describe our lives are important, they shape how we think. During the pandemic it seemed like many people were putting their lives on hold, waiting for things to get 'back to normal'. But what does that mean? It implies that it is desirable to return to a previous state. But sometimes that's impossible. Things have changed too much to go back to how they were before. For many of us, the last few years have highlighted that our lives were not well-balanced in the first place.

It might not be that one catalysing event has left us feeling off-kilter: it could be a crystallisation of discontent. By that I mean a period of unhappiness that has prompted a trans-formational life change, when we think to ourselves, *I can't take this anymore, things now must change.*

When we realise that we are off balance, it's time to look at life afresh. It is not helpful to try to go back to how things were; we need to work out how to rebalance ourselves and go forward. I have certainly experienced that myself.

The last few years may also have prompted all of us to ask questions about the directions of our lives. Are we living the life we want? Are we creating the right balance in our lives between all our different responsibilities and our interests at work and home? Have we been thinking about whether to change careers? Do we feel that we are living our lives to the full?

For each of us these are important questions. It is also typical for us to ask ourselves questions that reflect the stage of our lives. There are big decisions to make in our early adult life, around working out who we are and what we want. Other questions about purpose and meaning might arise in our mid-life as we seek to understand the direction our lives have taken and how to go forward.

In our later years, we may want to make sense of our journey and the contributions we have made and can now make for others. What questions we ask ourselves will also be shaped by our culture and the trends in our lives at the time. At the core of these questions is that we are seeking to make sense of what really matters to us. No one else can answer such significant questions for us. But it can be difficult to figure out the answers and how to move forward. It takes time to think these sorts of questions through. Sometimes, it seems easier to put the questions to the back of our minds to answer later. But as much as we might try to put such thoughts away, they will keep bothering us. These are the worries and concerns that in the silence of the small hours of the night, like an unwanted visitor, keep knocking at our doors.

A sense of irritation, boredom, monotony and routine is common for many of us, as are feelings of tension and anxiety. Such uncomfortable feelings may be that unanswered knocking at the door, and if we listen carefully enough, they will point us towards the much deeper issues that need exploring. The longer we ignore the knocking however, the louder it becomes. Our feelings then become overwhelming.

And if we ignore the knocking for too long, eventually the door may get kicked down.

Our uncomfortable feelings, whether of irritation, tension, anxiety or whatever, are telling us something. I believe it is the direction we need to go in. It is like our bodies are cleverer than our minds. We often can't think our way forward, but if we pay attention to our bodies and how we are feeling, we know the way. But we must be able to listen to ourselves and understand the language of feelings to know what direction to go in. It is learning to trust our gut. But not everyone has those skills well enough developed.

Many of us just struggle on, going round in circles trying to find answers for ourselves, confused about what direction to take. Others find someone like me to talk to, psychotherapists who will help them listen to themselves in a new and deeper way. Perhaps everything seems fine on the surface, but underneath there is a sense of discontent. Or there are problems – failing relationships, stalled careers, conflicts, feelings of upset. At first, people may say they just want to 'get back to normal', but psychotherapy helps us look at what's behind our concerns and to find new directions forward.

Psychotherapy is often thought of as an activity for curing people of psychological problems, and there is some truth to this, but we don't have to wait for a crisis. I think of it more often as a means to help us find our way in life.

Psychotherapy helps us become more fully functioning, but not just in terms of how well we conform to society's expectations and values – fully functioning in terms of becoming the best version of ourselves that we can be, and sometimes that might challenge social expectations and values.[2] If we are to be free to be ourselves, sometimes we must kick against the constraints that others put on us.

Psychotherapy, as I understand it, and will write about in this book, is ultimately a discussion about the good life and a vision of how to lead it. Psychotherapy helps us to explore ourselves and what life means to us. It is about learning to be ourselves, and to become free of our conditioning. As a psychotherapist, I see my role as helping us to untangle the knots in our thoughts and feelings. Then, we can begin to see the answers to our questions more clearly. What often happens next is that we come to realise our lives weren't really on track in the first place. Over months, or years, we can get to peel away the layers and find something deeper behind our discontent, identifying new understandings of what really matters. Getting back on track now means something much bigger.

But what? It means changing our priorities and perspectives and finding a new balance for ourselves in terms of the things that matter to us. I also think it involves us becoming more realistic about ourselves, honest in what we tell ourselves and more willing to take responsibility for ourselves. Most of the time, we are living in a deluded reality in which we behave as if we will live for ever, and as if what other people think about us is more important than what we think about ourselves. These realisations sometimes seem to come out of the blue – lightbulb moments in which people suddenly gain a new perspective on how to lead their lives. In the Zen Buddhist tradition, such an awakening has a name: *satori* – the experience of seeing into one's own true nature. It's about looking at life afresh.

In this book, I will share what I believe are the most important of these realisations: the six ways in which we can begin to see ourselves and the world anew, without distortion, and embark on a road to personal growth and a more emotionally mature life. These are often hard-earned lessons that come at great cost, such as illness or bereavement. When confronted by such adversity, we might then realise that what really matters to us is not so much the big things that we once thought were so important – our status and wealth, for example – but the things we took for granted, our health and companionship with others. But do we have to wait for adversity to strike to learn such lessons in life?

With an open mind, at the right time, such lessons can be learned by anyone. In my work, over three decades as a psychologist, psychotherapist, university professor and researcher, I have listened to stories of loss and trauma, conducted numerous research studies and taught many students the art of psychotherapy. In thinking about what I have learned and how to move forward in my own life, I have drawn on this experience. Using examples from my research and practice, I have distilled this vital knowledge to reveal what I see as the six things in life that really matter.

I encourage all of us to seek the answers to the questions that usually only confront people following adversity, and after many hours on a therapist's couch. Therapy can be one of the most wonderful experiences, but is it really necessary for change to occur? I believe not.

Over the years, I have come to believe that the six lessons I've focused on are often learned without therapy. I know from bitter experience that the unpleasant and unwanted trigger, often the spark that lights the fire of such personal growth and the search for the truth of who we are, can be difficult and even terrifying, as it challenges the image we have of ourselves.

Take, for example, how those who experience adversity often go through the same journey as therapy clients – but without the therapy. Imagine how illness can suddenly jolt a person to realise their days are precious. For them, *satori* doesn't spark from hours of therapy in which they slowly unravel their existing views about themselves, but from a sudden, unexpected and unwanted event that exposes the fragility of life, shattering their illusions and assumptions and setting in motion the same therapeutic process. In Zen

Buddhism, the term for this type of *satori* is called *kenshō*, which refers to growth that arises through pain and suffering, a moment of dramatic insight as opposed to the slower unfolding of our awareness that happens in therapy.

I am not saying that things always happen for a reason or that adversity always brings benefits. Of course not. It is also important to say that while there is truth in the idea that adversity can be a spark for personal growth for many people, it is not true for everyone, and even when it is, it may take many months or even years to happen. I know how painful loss can be and how difficult it can be for people to move forward in their lives. While no one would wish trauma upon themselves, we can reverse engineer what we know about how adversity can spark personal growth. Confronting mortality reroutes our attention to what really matters.

The inevitability of death is a topic that many of us avoid thinking about, but deliberately turning our attention towards it – reflecting on the shortness of our lives and the fragility of our existence – can be the most important first spark of personal growth. Such a view also echoes that of many cultures around the world. *Wabi sabi*, for example, refers to a more traditional Japanese way of life rooted in Zen Buddhism, that recognises a simple life in which we accept and appreciate the true nature of things. In her book *Wabi Sabi: Japanese Wisdom for a Perfectly Imperfect Life*,

self-help author Beth Kempton writes '... we are imper-
manent, just like everyone we love, and everything in the
world around us. We will not live for ever. We may not even
live a long time. Life is precious, and fleeting. It's up to us
to make the most of it at each stage, starting where we are
right now.'[3]

Psychologists have long known that there are different
stages that we go through in life. Our priorities at a young
age will be different to those of an older age. When we are
young, unless we have encountered death already, life seems
to stretch into the distance. When we are older, that same
distance now seen in the mirror seems but a short journey.
In this way, some of the lessons in this book, and what they
mean to us personally, will depend on where we are right
now in our own journey through life. While they all are
important lessons to learn at any age, we can only be open
to them when we are ready.

It can take a lifetime to learn these lessons. As we age, we
will experience time speeding up ever more until we may
feel ourselves hurtling towards the end. Only then may we
get closer to grasping how to lead life with greater wisdom.
But this can feel too late, leaving us with sadness and regret.
Sometimes this learning process seems accelerated when
the nature of life, the lessons to be learned, don't come slowly
in trickles over a lifetime, but come crashing through the
roof on a stormy night. What I have tried to do here is distil

some of that learning in ways that we can all benefit from before the stormy night befalls us.

For many of us, if we were to focus on what really matters, the fog that stops us seeing ourselves with openness and honesty would clear. For example, we might no longer be willing to always do what others expected of us or only be the people others wanted us to be. Instead, we would move towards self-direction. No longer content with the old certainties, we would become aware that our lives are an ever-changing adventure. Our eyes would be opened to the complexities of the world and ourselves as part of it. We would no longer be driven so much by 'oughts' and 'shoulds' but become more open to new experiences, seeking to learn, change and enjoy the challenges ahead. We would seek to understand ourselves and be the best versions of ourselves. We would begin to embrace the richness of life. We would become more trusting of ourselves and of others.[4] This is what psychotherapists mean when they talk about personal growth.

What allows such personal growth to take hold is self-acceptance. This is commonly understood as feeling good about oneself, but in this book, I refer to self-acceptance as a deeper and more profound way of thinking, when we can view our thoughts and feelings without reference to the attitudes or expectations of others or the rules and values of society. With that comes the ability to trust what our feelings tell us, to know what decisions are right or wrong for us and to take responsibility for our choices. Self-acceptance is the foundation stone for personal growth. Most of us in Western society, however, grow up encouraged to value material success, to please others to gain acceptance and to defer to those who have authority over us – all at the expense of our ability to be self-accepting.

Such lessons may seem obvious, but because they run counter to what most people have learned, they can be hard to implement. We simply aren't looking for *satori*. We want to change our lives, but we don't want to have to change ourselves. Yes, we can learn to change our habits or shift our mood – and there are many psychologists and therapies available that will help us do just that – but such changes in our lives will be superficial and short-lasting, unless we are also willing to change ourselves. Real therapeutic change involves thinking deeply about who we are and making the effort to peel away layers of denial, delusion and defence to reveal the emergence of a new version of who we are.

We read self-help books seeking wisdom for ourselves. Personal growth can arise through adversity, as I have mentioned, or through watching a sunset, climbing to the peak of mountain, witnessing the birth of a child, even sitting with someone in their final hours or any other number of human experiences, including reading a book that shifts how we see ourselves and the world around us.

Self-help books require an active role on the part of the reader, but this is not so different from therapy. Therapy gives us the opportunity to learn about being ourselves, but we must take what we learn in therapy into the world. I've heard it said that therapy is like starting a car, but you then must drive it. The realisations you may have through reading this book are no different: there may be some lightbulb moments, but life itself won't change in an instant. Like therapy, you must take what you learn in this book and put it into practice. Like reading a travel guide, you can choose some new and exciting options, see if they work and come back later for more ideas.

There is an old Zen proverb, 'When the student is ready the teacher will appear'. When we see a therapist for the first time, we may expect the therapist to do something to make us change. When the therapist doesn't that can feel frustrating. 'When is the therapy going to start?' we may ask. But the therapy has started – the therapist is deliberately not taking power away from us. And we are taking the first step, which is learning that we need to take responsibility ourselves for the change we want to make. The learning is in the shift of power from therapist to client. With that, we, the client, learn to use the resources we have around us to the best effect. We notice things that we hadn't noticed before and we see meanings where we previously hadn't. We begin to talk to the therapist, not like someone waiting to be told what to do, but like we are now seeking to understand the truth about ourselves and opening up to new possibilities.[5] It is in that sense the teacher will appear. When we are ready, we will find who or what we need to help us learn.

There is another famous Zen parable of the finger pointing at the moon. The finger is needed for us to know where to look, but the finger is not the moon. We need to look beyond the finger and not make the mistake of turning the finger itself into the object of our gaze. I feel that this is an apt metaphor for any book like this: all a writer can do is point to things, but it is up to the reader to look in the direction in which they are being pointed. I would ask you to take time in your reading. See through the words to the ideas and images that they represent, sit with these ideas and images and let them sink into your soul. Think about what they mean for you and your life, what you can begin to do differently. The things I am writing about are enormous and life-changing. If you are ready to let them be.

That is what this book offers. For some, it may be an alternative to therapy, for others it may be a companion to therapy, for still others it may be the beginning of a life-long therapeutic journey into becoming themselves. For deep personal change, we simply need the spark that lights the fire within us. It is a sad fact that it often takes some upsetting event in a person's life to be the spark that lights the fire of personal growth. But what is sadder perhaps is that we spend so much time unwittingly trying to put that fire out, as the search for the truth of who we are can be difficult and even terrifying. The principles in this book show how deep personal change can come about, and my hope is that it will open readers up to the possibilities within them.

I have organised the book around six inspirational and thought-provoking quotes that capture these principles. I have carefully selected each of these quotes. So, take your time to read them and think about their meaning. I don't claim to reveal any new truths about how to live life, but sometimes we all need to be reminded about what really matters. My intention has been to distil the most vital lessons out of the noise and chatter and that's what I have described as the six fundamental truths, as that is what they seem to me. Whether you agree is a question for only you to answer.

Each of us is on our own journey of personal growth and must take our own route. There is an old joke about a man who is travelling and who stops to ask a local person for directions. The local listens to the man's question, scratches his head, and says, 'Yes, I know where that is, and I can tell you how to get there, but I wouldn't start from here.' The message of the joke is, of course, that we all must start from where we are. That applies to this book. While the six truths I focus on are not wholly independent truths, as each seems to arise from the preceding one, and the chapters are arranged in a way that the book can be read from cover to cover, it may also be more useful for certain readers to dip in and out, according to interest and where you find yourselves in life, at the time of reading.

Writing this book has been an exercise in reminding myself what really matters, and I hope my efforts prove helpful to you, too. I would recommend keeping a journal by your side to jot down your thoughts, feelings and observations. Along the way, there will be questions for you, some exercises to try and some points for reflection. Writing can be an outlet for your feelings, helping you to explore honestly the reality of a situation and providing a way to connect with your inner wisdom. Engaging in writing in these creative ways can really help you to dig down and explore your thoughts and feelings in a new way.

In my own life I have found that sometimes all it takes is a helpful nudge in the right direction to get me going, a provocative quote or a question that stops me in my tracks and gets me to think again about something. It has become one of my greatest joys to recognise life as an unfolding story of personal development, emotional maturity and increased wisdom, and to become increasingly open to new possibilities in myself. I hope you can also find the same joys through this book.

1

Second Life

*'A person has two lives; the second
life begins when they realise
that they only have one.'*

The above quote is attributed to Confucius, the Chinese philosopher, but in recent years it has become more closely associated with Steven Sotloff, an American journalist who wrote about the Middle East.

After crossing the Syrian border from Turkey, on 4 August 2013, Sotloff was kidnapped by the Islamic State group. He was held in captivity for over a year, during which time his family and government officials tried to secure his release, without success. On 2 September 2014, he was murdered. The Islamic State posted a video online of him, kneeling and bound, being beheaded. At Sotloff's memorial, excerpts were read from a letter to his parents, which he had smuggled out of captivity, in which, paraphrasing the quote attributed to Confucius, he wrote: 'Everyone has two lives; the 2nd one begins when you realise you have only one.'[1] For me, these words convey the most significant truth that any of us will ever hear.

Steven Sotloff's life was ended before he had the opportunity to fully embrace the wisdom of his own words, but it is wisdom that is shared by many who confront terror and tragedy. The truth of the saying – how life seems to shine most brightly in the most troubled times – was revealed to me over thirty years ago in my work as a disaster psychologist.

In March 1987, the *Herald of Free Enterprise* left the port of Zeebrugge, Belgium, en route to England. Nearly 500 passengers, 80 crew and 1,100 tons of haulage were on board. Passengers were settling into their seats, queuing up at the restaurants and ordering drinks at the bar. Unbeknown to them, one of the bow doors had not been secured. Below, water was flooding on to the car decks. No one noticed anything was wrong until the ship attempted to turn. It lurched. Within forty-five seconds, the ship had rolled over.

There was no time to sound alarms of any kind. Furniture, cars, trucks and passengers were indiscriminately catapulted to port side. People collided with one another, crashed into walls and slipped under the ice-cold water as portholes imploded and water flooded the passenger areas. Electricity went out. The darkness reverberated with screams and shouts of pain and terror. Many thought they were going to die; many lost loved ones; many witnessed unimaginable horrors. One hundred and ninety-three people died in what was one of the most horrific maritime disasters of the twentieth century. It is hard to fathom what it must have been like to experience the *Herald* tragedy. Imagine the room you are in right now lurching and then suddenly turning upside down, throwing its contents from one side to the other. The ceiling becomes the floor, the lights go out and water starts flooding in.

A few months after the disaster, lawyers, acting on behalf of survivors and bereaved relatives, contacted the psychology department at the Institute of Psychiatry in London to ask for help. Survivors were visiting for psychological treatment, but at the time, little was known about the psychological effects of trauma and psychological treatment. This was a new field of psychology that was just opening up. That is how I became involved: as a doctoral researcher, my study was devoted to investigating the roadblocks to psychological recovery that survivors of trauma faced and what factors seemed to promote better outcomes. If we knew that, I felt, we might be able to develop new, more successful treatments.

In 1990, three years on from the disaster, my supervisor at the time, Professor William Yule, was developing a questionnaire to be sent out to all the survivors asking them about how they were doing at that point. While we knew many faced considerable difficulties in their lives at home and at work, we wanted to know the extent of the problems faced and how common they were.[2]

One day when we were talking about the survey and what questions to include, I mentioned that I had noticed during my earlier interviews with a small number of the survivors that some had talked about positive changes in their lives. I suggested that we also explore this. It seemed important to understand the possibility of positive changes, as perhaps it might give us a new clue as to how to help people. As a result, alongside the typical questions about psychological functioning that are often included in surveys with survivors of traumatic events, asking about anxiety, irritability and bad dreams, for example, we also included the question, 'Has your view of life changed since the disaster – and, if so, has it changed in a positive way or a negative way?' Squeezed into the survey at the last minute, it seemed like a controversial question to include: we didn't want people to think that we were downplaying what they had gone through or that we weren't taking them seriously. Survivors were asked to tick a box indicating if their view of life had changed for the worse, for the better or neither. The results were surprising. Although 46 per cent said that their view of life had changed for the worse, 43 per cent said that it had changed for the better.[3]

While my research started out being about the psychological difficulties people experienced, this one finding led me to spend the next two decades researching and studying how it is that people can grow following adversity. I wrote about this before in my book, *What Doesn't Kill Us*, in which I described my research over that time and how a positive outlook on life can unfold out of tragedy and trauma.[4] Indeed, my research helped spark interest in a new field of psychology into positive changes following adversity that came to be known as 'posttraumatic growth', a term coined by two American clinical psychology researchers based in North Carolina, Richard Tedeschi and Lawrence Calhoun.[5]

Posttraumatic growth refers to how people deal with trauma and turn it around into something positive for themselves. For example, people may find that their view of themselves changes in a way in which they recognise strengths in themselves that they hadn't realised before, begin to see their lives from a new and more meaningful perspective and value their relationships more deeply with others.

A brush with death will often spark posttraumatic growth. One of the very specific features of it is a greater appreciation of life, a recognition that it is precious and should not be squandered. Studies have shown, time and again, that events that confront people with their own mortality seem to be a springboard to positive changes in outlook. One study looked at cancer patients, most of whom had suffered either breast or testicular cancer, who all thought, at some point, they were going to die. They had finished their physical treatment and showed no signs of disease recurrence. Almost all agreed that they didn't take life or the people around them for granted anymore and valued their relationships more, and that they lived each day to the fullest.[6] Trauma can teach people what really matters to them and, more importantly, *who* really matters to them. I've since seen how adversity can be a turning point, not just as a researcher but also as a therapist who has listened to many stories of people who have endured life-threatening illnesses, harrowing natural disasters or horrific accidents.

Of course, the notion that confrontation with human frailty can be a stepping-stone to a wiser way of living is far from new. Confucius apart, the Greek philosopher and founder of Western philosophy Socrates recommended that we should 'always be occupied in the practice of dying'. Yet while a brush with death can be the first spark, does it really need to be a close brush in which we ourselves are threatened? Or do we simply need to open our eyes to the suffering around us? This is the foundation of the Buddhist tradition.

Prince Siddhartha Gautama grew up surrounded by all the pleasures of life and suffering was kept hidden from him. At sixteen, he married a beautiful princess and lived in his palace surrounded by comfort and luxury. As a young man in his late twenties, he left his home and embarked on a journey, during which he glimpsed the suffering of ordinary people. First, he met an old man, exhausted by a life of toil. Next, he met a man afflicted with a serious illness. Then, he saw a corpse being carried in a funeral procession surrounded by mourners. Finally, he encountered a holy man who helped him realise that old age, sickness and death are inevitable – even for those who have had the happiest and most prosperous of lives. Aware that his life in the palace was not an answer to the problem of human suffering, Gautama left his kingdom. He studied for six years with spiritual teachers, without finding the answers to his questions. He sat beneath a Bodhi tree and resolved not to eat or to leave until he reached enlightenment, even if death was the result. At the age of thirty-five, after deep and prolonged meditation, he eventually reached enlightenment and became the Buddha.[7]

The term Buddha is not a name but rather a title that means 'one who is awake'. The Buddha claimed that he was merely a man who had achieved a greater understanding of human existence. He taught for the next forty-five years, travelling from town to town in India, and died at the age of eighty. Buddhism holds that, in existence, everything is constantly changing, and therefore suffering is inevitable. Most of us do not grow up in a palace like the prince, but we do go through life as if our time were an unlimited resource, pushing thoughts of death to the side. But in fact, our lives are like an hourglass, with the sands of time unstoppable in their flow.

As mentioned earlier, the Buddhist term *kenshō* refers to a deep insight that arises through suffering, in which someone sees and understands the true nature of reality. In modern psychology, we call this posttraumatic growth, for many years my main interest as a psychologist. What I found so intriguing about this phenomenon is how familiar it is, in the sense that everyone recognises the truth of it, at least intellectually. Yet most of us fail to live by this truth, at least until we ourselves have a real encounter with death.

It is curious that we are a culture that generally hides death in hospitals in such a way that many of us will not encounter it until we ourselves are in middle age, or even later, and then it is often through the death of a parent. It might be through spending time with them in their final moments – peaceful or a time of great anguish and suffering for them. For many of us, it may be a glimpse into the nature of existence that we have not seen before.

Why is it that we fail to appreciate the full value of our health, the people we love, our peace, freedom and prosperity, and even life itself, until they are taken away from us through a sudden illness, accident or injury? Why only then do we experience the depth of knowing – not just intellectually, but in our bones?

Such a heightened appreciation of life can seem to come at too high a cost. As Charlotte Delbo, who described her experience during the Holocaust in *Auschwitz and After*,[8] wrote:

> *I've spoken with death*
> *and so*
> *I know*
> *the futility of things we learn*
> *a discovery I made at the cost*
> *of a suffering*
> *so intense I keep on wondering*
> *whether it was worth it*

Is it better to go through life avoiding all encounters with suffering but, as a result, never achieving a full appreciation of being alive? Or is it better to suffer the losses that would lead to a more appreciative life? These are good questions to ask ourselves, but thankfully it is not a choice that we will ever have to make. Suffering is inevitable, as the Buddha says. Our only real choice is in how we approach it when it happens.

*

As a specialist in trauma therapy, I felt defeated at how my research studies only ever seemed able to indicate how to help people *after* tragedy. As important as this is, what really intrigued me was the question of how a more appreciative life might be developed without having first gone through such suffering.

Psychotherapists, by definition, wait downstream for tragedies, misfortunes and losses to happen, as that is what brings clients to our door. But I wanted to travel upstream, to think about how the wisdom from my research could be applied to those who have not yet encountered trauma. As I thought about this, the answer seemed obvious. Encounters with suffering and mortality await all of us, but we also don't need to wait for the hand of death to rest on our shoulder before finding a way to live a more appreciative life. The key is to spend time reflecting on our own mortality.

'Mortality salience' is the term used to describe when we become aware of the possibility of our own death. We generally tend not to do this in everyday life, and we often make great efforts to avoid it, but we do come to mortality salience every so often through unanticipated moments of meaning. We can also, of course, consciously choose to think about it. I am not talking here about the big events in life that befall us – the tragedies, misfortunes and losses – but the opportunities along the way, which may otherwise go unnoticed, that allow us to glimpse our mortality. Evidence from research by Laura Carstensen, a Stanford psychologist, shows that our perception of the time we have left in life guides our motivations. When we perceive a lot of time ahead, like when we are young and death seems unthinkably distant, we focus on our careers, our wealth and our status. The research also tells us that when the time left to live feels shorter, and we feel death getting closer, our attention shifts to value the people and relationships in our lives and to seek more emotionally meaningful pursuits.[9]

Many of us seem to live life on the surface, going from one activity to the next, doing what is required of us in our various roles, as if we were sleepwalking. It can be exhausting, and it may not bring us much pleasure or give us much sense of meaning. In the evenings, maybe we lose ourselves for a while in television, with some chocolate or with a bottle of wine. Perhaps we promise ourselves that some time in the future our lives will be different when we find our real calling.

Moments of awakening, or *kenshō*, are rare, but these are times when we feel that we have seen the true nature of reality. It might sound like they are moments where something extraordinary happens to you. In fact, it may be in the context of the most ordinary and everyday events that such moments arise. I can remember one occasion where I narrowly avoided death. Immediately afterwards, I felt more alive, more awake and more present. I felt so blessed to still be alive and to have more time to complete the things I wanted to do and especially to see those I loved.

I was just going about my everyday business, doing some home maintenance work. It was a very ordinary day, during which I dismantled an old built-in wardrobe. After, I drove to the recycling centre and was throwing the heavy wooden boards into a skip which was situated over a wall about ten feet below. What I hadn't paid attention to was that inside the wardrobe there had been lengths of electric wiring that were still attached to different parts of the dismantled wardrobe. As I threw one piece of timber, a flat piece of wood that it was still attached to it flew up from behind me, scraping my neck on its way past me into the skip. I stood there afterwards in the realisation of just how close I had come to slicing my own throat wide open. I still shiver when I think about it.

What is remarkable is that this event is in one way so trivial, but at the same time, acted as a powerful reminder to me of how close to the edge we always are, and how such moments can strike at any time. You may have had something similar happen to you.

There are a number of other times that I've been similarly lucky, but this close escape stays with me in my memory because of the shift in perspective I had immediately afterwards. What I realised was how that sense of the closeness of death left me with a sense of contentment, a deeper appreciation that I was alive, and how it could be so much more meaningful to live a life in full awareness of one's mortality. Most of the time we go about our daily business with the thought of our own death tucked away comfortably in the back of our minds, but what seems more enriching is when we use it to see things afresh and with new perspective. I wanted to find a way to hold on to this vital awareness and not let it fade.

My experiences led me to think about how we can choose to make moments of meaning, to deliberately seek out events that are different from those of our daily lives, to provoke a more mixed reaction of emotions with the intention of learning about ourselves in some way. I started taking this seriously almost twenty years ago. I was coming up to my fortieth birthday, which at the time seemed like a landmark age. Friends were asking what I would do to celebrate, but I didn't feel like doing so. At the time, I was going through an unhappy period in my life, but as a psychologist I knew what the problem was. I had become too caught up in the material world, worried about my career, success, wealth – all the things that we know lead to unhappiness. I knew what I needed to do, and that was an exercise that would help me gain perspective. So, after thinking about what to do to mark the occasion, my wife and I decided to visit the Auschwitz concentration camp in Poland. So, there were no cakes or candles: instead we spent the day thinking about others, those who had been lost during the Holocaust, all the lives that had been cut short so brutally.

My trip to the Auschwitz concentration camp was also important to me as someone with Jewish ancestry. I had grown up in the shadow of the Second World War and its horrors and had experienced antisemitism; it was all too common when I was young to hear the word 'Jew' used as an insult. It felt right to spend that time reflecting on those horrific events and thinking of the people who had suffered there and elsewhere during that terrible time last century, but the trip was also important for my growth as a human being. At that time in my life, I needed to find a way to transcend my everyday personal concerns and see myself and my place in the world from a wider perspective.

To me, it felt right at that time to deliberately do something that would provoke something deeper and more enriching in my appreciation of life and its significance. At forty, a turning-point age in my life, I wanted to be pointed in the direction of a life that would have more value and that would come about by thinking about others rather than myself.

That was almost two decades ago, but it is this process of personal growth that I have since come to understand and value so much in myself, my clients and my students that I wish to share here. The quote with which I opened this chapter cuts through our self-deception to provoke us into realising how much more we can make of our lives. When we consciously face the prospect of our own demise, it can set us on a different path. For me, it seems that choosing to embark on the journey of learning about ourselves now is the greatest kindness we can show to our future selves. When I think of death now, I fear the prospects of ill health, loneliness and incapacity that I have seen others go through in their final days, but death itself is not frightening, at least in the way it once was. What now seems so much more urgent is living a life that is fuller and gives me the experiences of being true to myself. That, I think, is the nature of personal growth. We discover some meaning for ourselves, perhaps by accident and, in that discovery, we are prompted to seek out more. Like the flowering of a blossom, meaning unfolds and opens within us over time as we encounter new experiences in life.

We are all, always, precariously balanced between life and death, surrounded by reminders of our mortality just one step away. But despite this, the profound lesson that our mortality has to teach us is easily overwhelmed by day-to-day concerns.

Existential philosophers have long talked about the sheer terror of facing our own mortality, such that we build our lives around the illusion that we are invulnerable and immortal. We structure our lives around this illusion and use our mental energy to fend off the truth that bad things could befall us at any minute. But sometimes the truth comes crashing through, and in those moments, we have the opportunity to see beyond the illusory world we have built for ourselves.

The truth is being a human being is a terrifying thing. To be born and then to grapple with life and impending death are so frightening that we can't stand it. Death looms over us all the time – it is too much, too overwhelming, too frightening, too puzzling. This is looked at in Terror Management Theory (TMT), a branch of psychology research developed by Jeff Greenberg, Sheldon Solomon and Tom Pyszczynski and expanded in their 2015 book, *The Worm at the Core*, which proposes that death anxiety drives people to adopt a worldview that protects and defends them from facing reality.[10] TMT says that when thoughts of death are in our awareness, we attempt to remove them from our consciousness by suppressing such thoughts, denying the threat or engaging in behaviour to reduce our sense of vulnerability.

I am reminded of the Buddhist story about a man who was walking across a field when he sees a tiger coming towards him. Immediately, he runs, but not looking where he is going, he goes over the edge of a cliff. Falling, he quickly grabs a vine. Safe for now, but hanging from the vine, he can see the tiger above him looking down and another tiger below looking up. Then, two mice start to gnaw at the vine. At this moment, the man sees a delicious-looking strawberry growing close by. Holding the vine with one hand, he plucks the strawberry. What does this story teach us? One lesson is that our lives are precarious, death is inevitable and all we can do is to make the most of the present moment. Take pleasure and enjoy what is good about life while you can. Imagine, if we lived forever, we could do all the things we ever dreamed of: there would always be time. But the fact of death sets limits and teaches us to see time as the precious commodity it is, to be enjoyed.

Another lesson from this fable, however, is the folly of letting ourselves be distracted by pleasure, such that we avoid facing reality. Perhaps this is the more important lesson: to not only be aware that life is limited but to reflect on how we spend that precious time. Are we like the man reaching for the strawberry, distracting ourselves from our mortality with momentary pleasures? Is that what we are doing when we sit on the couch in the evenings watching TV and eating chocolate?

According to TMT, a lot of our life choices are actually distractions to help us deal with death anxiety. By the latter, I mean the dread and fear that people have of the spectre of their own or another's demise and the process of dying. Our routines and rituals, the ambitions and careers we pursue, are all inventions that allow us to give meaning to our lives in what is really a meaningless world, allowing us to believe we play an important role in some way. But they are essentially distractions from our death anxiety and the truth that it is a meaningless world. That might sound like a hopeless thing to say, but I don't mean it like that. Rather, it is about recognising that the meaning of our lives isn't given to us: we make meaning for ourselves.

TMT is not a new idea. It is based on earlier work by the sociologist Ernest Becker, who argued in his 1973 book, *The Denial of Death*, that most human actions are a way to ignore our mortality.[11] He wrote: 'It is fateful and ironic how the lie we need in order to live dooms us to a life that is never really ours'. Is it possible that our lives – directed towards success and the pursuit of power and wealth – are actually, deep down, motivated by an unconscious equation that says success, power and wealth are paths to invincibility, and that all we are doing is defending ourselves against death fears? The answer is yes. For Becker, we need to suppress our awareness of our fragility, of the fact that we are always only a split second away from non-existence, otherwise we would simply go mad. And so, we develop cultures that make us feel invulnerable and eternal – what Becker called 'immortality systems'. The various different religions all provide ideas about life after death that serve this purpose, and are examples of immortality systems: those routines, rituals and possessions that allow us to give a sense of meaning to our lives and avoid our death anxiety. We each find our own way to find this reassurance. I look back on my own career as a university professor with all its ceremony and procedures, and I feel I can glimpse this for myself. As I look around my office at the stacks of books and journals that surround me, I can feel reassured, albeit falsely, that the world is a safe and meaningful place.

It is just too much for people to face reality. It is too terrifying. The French writer La Rochefoucauld famously said that death, like the sun, cannot be looked at steadily. Irvin Yalom adapted this saying as the title for his book *Staring at the Sun*, in which he argued that we can indeed look at death, and that we are better for doing so than not.[12] I would agree, but it may be hard to look at it directly for too long, which is why we look at it indirectly, in the only ways we can, through music, poetry and religion, such that we can live our lives keeping death at a comfortable distance and go about our daily business.

One of the ways we allow ourselves to look at death out of the corner of our eye is through horror movies and novels. Indirectly, we may allow ourselves to confront our deepest existential fears from the safety of the sofa. But perhaps we even make it more of our daily business to look at death more directly, as I feel I did when I specialised as a trauma psychologist, confronted as I was every day by stories of unimaginable loss and encounters with death. Of course, all the daily business that consumes us, our ambitions, desires and so on, may seem like nothing one day when we ourselves stare directly and steadily at death.

On the surface, it seems obvious enough that death is threatening and that we do things to avoid thinking about it. But it can be enriching and create meaning in our lives to – metaphorically – look at the sun every so often. To do so can be a profound shake-up of how we perceive ourselves and the world around us. By peeling back the layers of our life – our values, opinions, beliefs – we can see that at the core of who we think we are, is a fear of death and a need to distort reality and deny that our lives are based on an illusion about what matters.

All of this seems so true to me now, writing in my late fifties, knowing that my life is closer to its end than its beginning. All the triumphs, defeats, successes and failures of my life, which seemed so important at the time, fade into the background and lose their significance – like how children moving into adolescence and young adulthood just stop playing with their toys. As we age and come closer to death and the frailties of human existence, understanding that life is to be lived with an appreciation of the moment and the joys of the simple things becomes clearer.

In his letter to his parents, journalist Steven Sotloff, wrote: 'Do what makes you happy. Be where you are happy. Love and respect each other. Don't fight over nonsense. Hug each other every day. Eat dinner together. Live your life to the fullest and pray to be happy. Stay positive and patient'.

Significant moments in our lives are often only seen in

the rear mirror. They are rarely understood as significant at the time. I think of the last time I saw a friend before his tragic death, unaware that it was to be our last meeting. Everything in our lives will come to an end but rarely are we given notice. How much wiser it would be to heed such advice in advance. It is my belief that a greater appreciation of death, and therefore of life, leads to an upward spiral of appreciation, something which Sotloff illustrates so powerfully in his letter. Death awareness promotes a sense of togetherness, that we all share the same fate and have the same fears, leading us to be kinder and more compassionate towards our fellow humans.

Read each of the statements below. How many do you think describe the type of person you are? Don't spend too much time thinking about your answer.

1. I'm the type of person who often reflects on how fortunate they are.
2. I'm the type of person who feels awestruck when they see natural beauty.
3. I'm the type of person who uses personal rituals to remind themselves to be thankful.
4. I'm the type of person who can stop and enjoy life as it is.
5. I'm the type of person who, when I see others who are less fortunate, realises how lucky I am.

6. I'm the type of person who says 'thank you' to
   show my appreciation and means it.
7. I'm the type of person who often reflects on how
   important my friends and family are to me.

If you thought all seven statements sounded like you,
then you already have a very appreciative personality,[13]
but typically only a few statements will ring true for most
people. Many of us have room to develop our ability to lead
an appreciative life.

When we look to the future, we may feel overwhelmed
with the anticipation of grief. Everyone we love will come
to an end. It may seem easier to live a life in which there
is no one to grieve for. It is one reason some of us keep
others at an emotional distance, but that is not living an
abundant life. To live a good life in the time left to us, the
avoidance of death is not an option. The more death is
avoided, the harder we must work to keep it at bay using all
our defences. And that stops us living in the present. The
way to embrace the presence of death is to build appreciation behaviours, rituals and habits into our lives, in such
a way as to provoke, to a manageable degree, a confrontation with our own mortality. I say manageable, because
as I've already mentioned, the threat of death anxiety is
a real thing, and too much confrontation too quickly is
terrifying. Instead, we can learn to turn mortality from

something we routinely deny, into something we are always aware of.

On one of my favourite regular walks, I pass a gravestone that has a quote from Proverbs 27:1. *'Do not boast about tomorrow, for you do not know what a day may bring forth.'* I take a route deliberately to pass this gravestone, which has become like an old familiar friend to me and always raises a smile. It reminds me that life is short and not to take it for granted. I stop for a few minutes on the bench nearby and reflect on the proverb and its meaning. I think of all those I have known who I have lost over the years, especially friends whose lives were cut short, and I think about the effect my death will have on others. My thoughts often wander in such a way as to lead me to develop more appreciative feelings. Some days, I think about my relationships with others, prompting me to feel more compassionate and loving towards them and realising how forgetful I may have become. On other days, I embrace a different view on what is happening in my life, and things that seemed so important just minutes ago are put into perspective. I may become less focused on myself and what others think of me and realise the strengths within myself.

Visiting a cemetery might seem like an odd way to spend an hour of an afternoon, but it is more common that you might imagine. Various cemeteries are popular destinations for tourists, such as Highgate in north London, famous for Karl Marx's tomb, or Père Lachaise in Paris, which contains the graves of Frédéric Chopin, Marcel Proust, Oscar Wilde and Jim Morrison, among others. These are garden cemeteries, designed for people to visit for walks, to appreciate nature, while being with their dead, or not even their own dead. Such places are interesting, and they can provide a contemplative space for us, as do other destinations such as the National Memorial Arboretum and the National Holocaust Centre and Museum in England or Arlington National Cemetery and the Holocaust Memorial Museum in the United States. Each of these places offers the opportunity for profound moments of reflection. But any place that allows us to transcend our own concerns for a while, to reflect on our own mortality and gain an appreciation of life, is helpful. Often you will see in graveyards these words inscribed on tombstones.

> *Remember friend as you walk by*
> *As you are now so once was I*
> *As I am now you will surely be*
> *Prepare thyself to follow me.*

Each person can find their own way to keep mortality in mind. Bob Harrison is a visiting professor at the University of Wolverhampton in England. In an interview, he told me about how, as a young man, in 1989, he attended a football match with his sons at Hillsborough Stadium in Sheffield to watch Liverpool play Nottingham Forest. Tragedy unfolded that day: because of poor crowd control, spectators were caught in a stampede and ninety-six people died in the crush. To this day, Bob says he remains haunted by some of the sights he saw but also that it made him realise that life is precious. 'That's what Hillsborough did, it sharpens your mind, it's rammed right in front of your face that you are going to die'. Thirty-two years later, he says he still carries the ticket for that game in his wallet to remind him of how precious his family is to him.

Reminders of mortality are all around us. Is there a daily ritual or something you could carry or do that might serve to gently prompt you each day to focus your thoughts on what really matters for you?

It is common for people who have lost a loved one to carry on talking with them, whether the person believes in some way that the conversation is real or imagined, people often find it of therapeutic value. If you have lost someone close this will likely not be a surprise to you, but it might be helpful to know that it is such a common thing to do. That is what Sandra Dannenbaum and Richard Kinnier of Arizona State University found when they interviewed older people who had experienced the loss of a loved one. Their research showed that despite it being something people often do, it is also something that people tend not to mention to others.[14] I often talk to my own parents in this way or friends who have died and, if I have a question to ask, it can help me find new perspectives. We can often imagine what that person might have said. Something similar is what some therapists might do, by asking people to imagine a conversation with someone who is not in the room, maybe asking them to move between two chairs as they say what they want to say from one chair, and then responding as they imagine what the other person might say from the other chair.[15]

Thinking about one's own mortality seems to confer some benefits for personal growth. In research by Laura Blackie and her colleagues at the University of Nottingham,[16] people were asked to imagine themselves dying, then to describe the life that they would have had up to that point and how their families would react. Their findings showed that engaging in the exercise provoked a greater sense of meaning and purpose. If you were to imagine your own death, how would you describe the life that you have had up to now? Take a few minutes to think about your answer.

Imagining our own death can be a helpful exercise. I remember seeing Julia, who scored very high on measures of depression, describe living her life in fear of something bad happening. She would hear her friends describe their holidays, adventures and trips to exotic places, but none of that was ever for her. She tried to keep herself safe, but she knew that she was missing out on life. Her evenings were spent in front of the television, comfort eating, by herself. Occasionally she would go out with friends, but she found those nights stressful. She would worry about losing her keys, travelling to the venue and back safely and the possibility of being robbed while she was out. She would feel relief just to get home. This had been her pattern for many years, and obviously it was working for her on some level to help her cope with her feelings of anxiety and stress, which was what seemed to keep this pattern going. But at another level, the sense of purposelessness and meaninglessness of her life seemed to be overwhelming, and after talking about it for several sessions she said to me, 'It's like I may as well be dead already.' We sat together to consider this statement and its paradoxical nature: that the things she was doing to keep herself alive and safe meant that she felt like she was dead. For Julia, this was a profound moment. We got to talking about death, what it meant to her and its inevitability.

Something about the conversation, and the fact that it was nearly Christmas, prompted me to mention *A Christmas Carol*, Charles Dickens's story about Ebenezer Scrooge, a miserly man whose life was devoted to money. On Christmas Eve, he is visited by three ghosts, including the ghost of 'Christmas yet to come'. The ghost gets Scrooge to look into the faces of lost loved ones, to contemplate future losses and to witness life after his own death. He is taken to visit his grave. Running his fingers over his name engraved on the tombstone, he is transformed. Awakening on Christmas morning, Scrooge is a new person. Now, no longer chained by greed as his sole purpose in life, he awakens to compassion and kindness to others. The remarkable thing is that, however many times we hear that story, it doesn't quite sink in until we each have our own experience of a near miss. We know what really matters in life, but our head forgets to tell our heart.

Inspired by Scrooge's story, I asked Julia to imagine what her own headstone would say if she were to die tomorrow. Without hesitation, she simply said, 'Loser'. We talked some more, and I asked Julia to now say what she would like her headstone to read. 'Loved by family and friends', she said. We sat in silence for some minutes. I could see that Julia was becoming tearful, but she didn't seem overwhelmed by her feelings. Rather, a steely determination seemed to have set in. This session, after several months together, proved to be a turning point for Julia.

Often, our lives are driven by ideas of success based on wealth, accolades or doing better than someone else, but rarely when asked to think about our headstone are these the things that come to mind. Thinking about our headstone challenges us to question our culturally conditioned narrative of what matters in life and focuses our mind on what we value.

What would the words on your headstone say? Don't think about your answer; just say whatever words come to mind. Are these the words you would like to see? Chances are you haven't ever given much thought to this and what you would like to be remembered for. Now take some time to think about what you would like your headstone to say.

Imagining death helps us to focus on what really matters and to set new goals that are truer to our values. I am not advocating that anyone ruminate endlessly on their own demise – that doesn't sound healthy – but that you find your own way to approach it in yourself and use it constructively to engage with life. This requires the ability to sit mindfully with your thoughts of mortality, observing and acknowledging your feelings and reflecting on their meaning for you.

The more you can confront your own mortality without provoking anxiety in yourself, the more you can deepen your exploration and create meaning by imagining the circumstances of your own death. Remember, I'm talking about doing this while you are still healthy as a way of promoting your own personal development. None of us know what will happen, but you can imagine different circumstances – especially the sights, smells, tastes and people you would want at your funeral. What songs would you like to have played or sung? Who would you like to make a speech? Imagine what your good death would be like. Perhaps you will want to write it down or talk to a friend or family member about it.

Perhaps the most obvious way to help confront your own mortality is thinking about the paperwork and making sure you have a will written. Sitting down to think about what will happen after your death, how it will affect others and how you want your assets to be apportioned is important. This is not about great wealth, as even the smallest gift can mean so much to someone as a memento of what they meant to you. In the process of making out a will, we learn what others mean to us.

As I come to the end of this chapter, I want to emphasise that I am not proposing for a second that anyone should become overly focused on their mortality and spend their days thinking about nothing else. Rather I feel that by allowing ourselves to be aware of death sooner rather than later, it can wake us up to what really matters in life, nudge us to live a more appreciative life and enable us to spend our time doing things that we might look back on with some satisfaction. Paradoxically, the more we acknowledge death is lurking behind us, the more it can prompt us to have healthier habits in eating, sleeping and exercise as ways to contribute to a longer, healthier, happier life. As a poem by Steven Shorrock reminds us:

> *No-one ever died wishing*
> *They'd stayed longer at the office*
> *Tapping at keys and staring at screens*
> *Sand trickling away into corporate machines*[17]

Finally, I will leave you with a question that some researchers have used to help people think about the meaningful moments in their lives. Imagine there is an afterlife in which all your earthly memories will be forgotten, except for one. What is the one memory from your life that you would choose to take with you? Ponder on that memory and what it tells you about what you value. Awareness of your own mortality can teach you the answer to the question of what you truly love and start you on the road to a more appreciative life. Such an awareness may motivate you to make wiser decisions, giving you the courage to lead a life of your own choosing.

Steve Jobs in his commencement address to students at Stanford said: 'Remembering that I'll be dead soon is the most important tool I've ever encountered to help me make the big choices in life. Because almost everything – all external expectations, all pride, all fear of embarrassment or failure – these things just fall away in the face of death, leaving only what is truly important. Remembering that you are going to die is the best way I know to avoid the trap of thinking you have something to lose. You are already naked. There is no reason not to follow your heart.'[18]

Jobs was right about this. His view that it is external expectations that hold us back in life is one that psychologists throughout the years have talked about. And it is this topic to which I will turn in the next chapter.

2

Accept Yourself

*'The curious paradox is that
when I accept myself just as
I am, then I can change.'*

Recently I was listening to the writer Edna O'Brien being interviewed on the BBC Radio 4 programme *Desert Island Discs*. Always drawn towards being a writer, she spoke about how she felt suffocated by a strict upbringing in rural Ireland in the 1940s, and how she was discouraged from pursuing her ambition. Somehow, despite this, and to the benefit of so many of us who have found joy and inspiration in her work, O'Brien found her direction in life and became a writer. Listening to that interview got me thinking about what it is that gives some people, but not others, the freedom to find their own direction in life. To answer that question I turned to Carl Rogers, the author of the opening quote, and one of the most influential psychotherapists of the last century. Rogers' lifetime's work was devoted to just this question, and for him, the answer was self-acceptance.

Rogers was a pioneer of psychotherapy and responsible for developing many of the ideas that we now take for granted. In essence, he said that the way in which we accept ourselves or not, goes back to what happens in our childhood. Childhood, he said, was a time when we become conditioned to see ourselves in a certain way, and most importantly, whether we regard ourselves in a positive light or not. He thought that much of human unhappiness was because people did not regard themselves positively.

Most people would agree that it is important to make sure that children have a high positive regard for themselves, and that those children who struggle to regard themselves positively are likely to go on to experience problems as adults. But what Rogers also said was that there are two types of self-regard. The first is what he called 'conditional self-regard' and the second, 'unconditional self-regard'. Conditional self-regard is when our feelings of worthiness depend on how much we look to other people to value us, whereas unconditional self-regard is when our feelings about ourselves are not dependent on what others think, but on our own internal compass. What Rogers promoted was the idea that we should help children to develop unconditional, rather than conditional, self-regard.[1] But it is the latter that more often happens.

The idea that our dreams can be crushed in childhood by those whose role is to nurture and care for us will be familiar to many. Our wishes, dreams and aspirations are ignored, laughed at and dismissed. No doubt, it is not always the intention to crush a child's dreams. More often, perhaps, those adults do so out of a misplaced desire to help. It may be that they genuinely think they are helping us by controlling and directing our lives. They want the best for us, but as seen from their point of view. They might then try to steer our lives in the direction that they think is right for us. As a result, we may learn that to be valued by them, we must head in that direction. Conditional regard can be very psychologically damaging when it works at cross purposes to the child's own directions in life. But even when consistent with the child's own directions, it may still be damaging, because it undermines the child's own internal motivation. This is called the 'overjustification effect', which is when an external incentive such as money or praise decreases a person's intrinsic motivation to perform a task.[2]

That is not to say that conditional regard cannot be the fuel to a very successful life in some ways, and many parents do use conditional regard to push their children to achieve distinction in sports or exams, for example, with what looks like great success. But no matter how successful a person may appear, if the direction they have travelled is not truly their own, can it really ever be the road to a good life? Research findings would seem to say not. When there are large discrepancies between people's ideals of what they want for their lives and what they actually achieve, we might expect them to be consumed with distressing feelings of regret.[3]

For a young person to develop unconditional self-regard, parents or other caregivers must provide their child with unconditional regard and the freedom to go in other directions to those that the parents would choose. We should not mistake good intentions for good actions. Unconditional parenting starts with the belief that each person is unique in what they bring to the world and that the duty of those who care is to help that person achieve their full potential. To do that we have to listen carefully to children, understand their point of view, their wishes and desires and do our best not to control and direct their lives, but empower and free them to find their own path. Parents who understand this show interest in their children, they listen to their children to find out what interests them to understand what it is like to be them. They value the individuality of their children and give them the freedom to be themselves and not someone that they want them to be. They let their children find their own path in life. All this does not imply passively looking on; they are parents who will get involved practically, offer advice and emotional support, but always do so in a way that enhances their child's ability to choose for themselves. Finally, they understand that their child's world is not their world. Children need to feel safe and secure, to feel it's OK to make mistakes and feel free to be creative and playful. Each child needs the space to express their unique talents and interests.

Parents and caregivers have an important role to play, but they often face an uphill battle against the conditional regard that children get in schools. Despite the best intentions of many teachers, the education system is rigged to promote conditional self-regard. Think about how schoolchildren are put on an endless treadmill of exams and tests. Children learn that doing well at school is important. Not surprisingly, many come to equate doing well at school with their self-worth. But the range of skills that are measured in the exams and tests are so narrow when compared to the wide range of all the abilities, talents and dreams of children. Some will feel left out and unvalued or that they are failures. But even those that do well are learning to only value themselves in this narrow way. It is incredible to realise how damaging the educational system is for many young people, and how long-lasting those effects are. You may indeed know it for yourself, but it remains something that is rarely talked about.

It is over forty years since I was at school, but I recall a time in my life where rewards seemed to go only to those who did well at exams and were good at sports. In particular, sport seemed to provide an opportunity for humiliating children. I remember the two best footballers were asked to pick their teams. In turn, they chose from the rest of us. We waited for our names to be called, feeling more worthless the longer we stood there. I remember one or two teachers as being kind, but many used mockery and shame as tools of teaching. At least that is how I remember my school years. I was learning how to behave and who I needed to become in order to be accepted by others, but I wasn't learning to accept myself. I certainly didn't feel that I had the opportunity to really find out what my abilities and talents in life were and develop them, which is what I now think school should be about for each child. It took me many years afterwards to learn to be able to take physical exercise without feeling worthless, so linked had the two become in my mind. Looking back, I had an unhappy time at school, but issues of mental health were not of the same concern back then as today.

Thankfully, we now pay more attention to the mental health of children, although unfortunately it seems to me that the emphasis is on providing help and therapy for them once they develop problems, rather than doing something about an educational system that provokes the problems in the first place. My impression is that for young people today, the demands on them are even greater.

Through awarding gold stars, we get children to follow the rules. But whose rules are they? They are the regulations of a system designed to produce conformity. I don't think it is surprising that recent estimates suggest that unhappiness is common among children and that substantial numbers suffer from depression and anxiety.[4]

Imagine what children go through in school with all the tests and competition to succeed. They are learning what they need to do to be winners or losers. But when do we stop to question the very assumption that life should be about winning or losing, that it is right to teach children that this competitive and materialistic way is how to think about life? The education system in Western society is geared towards career preparation, but is that all education should be about? Why do we not think of education as more than that? It could be about helping young people develop their understanding of themselves, their emotions and their relationships, with the aim of preparing them for their lives rather than simply their jobs.[5] Imagine an education system that was not based on races, applause and gold stars, but designed to help young people discover their unique abilities and talents. To find a way to lead a truly flourishing life. What if children were valued for who they were, unconditionally?

As social beings, we are a product of the messages we internalise from the world around us, especially when we are young, and our minds are receptive and easily influenced. Each generation grows up learning what is supposed to matter. Thinking about this, and your own experiences, what would you say to yourself if you were able to write a letter from you as you are now, to you when you were eleven years old? What advice would you give the younger you?

There is such a lot of pressure on young people to act as the person they need to be to get the love and affection they seek, but over time it ceases to be a performance: it becomes who they are. Many years later, as adults, we are still trying to be the person we needed to be back then. Even though those we sought to please may be no longer in our lives, maybe even dead, we still have the remnants of their voices in our heads. We accept ourselves only through the eyes of others.

Coming into the present, thinking about your own self-regard, how much would you agree with the following statements?

- I treat myself in a warm and friendly way.
- I feel that I appreciate myself as a person.
- I have a lot of respect for myself.

If you agree with those statements, then it seems likely that you have a positive regard for yourself, but how conditional is your regard? What about the following statements?

- Whether other people criticise me or praise me makes no real difference to the way I feel about myself.
- How I feel towards myself is not dependent on how others feel towards me.
- Whether other people are openly appreciative of me or openly critical of me, it does not really change how I feel about myself.

If you agree with those statements,[6] then it seems likely that you take an unconditional attitude towards yourself, and that your self-regard is dependent on your own internal compass, rather than looking to others for approval, vindication or validation. I hope that sounds like you. Such people tend to feel free to be themselves, are comfortable in their own skin and able to find their own directions in life unencumbered by the values and expectations of others. And research shows that they tend to have more self-compassion, score lower on measures of depression and anxiety and higher on measures of well-being.[7]

To be able to accept ourselves and give ourselves the love and acceptance for who we are regardless of our faults and successes is key to a happy life, and the greatest gift that we can give ourselves or someone else. But it is a rare quality. Most of us, most of the time, seem to be more conditional in our regard for ourselves. Psychologists of all persuasions agree with how destructive it is for us when our self-worth is conditional on others' approval. A person can appear to have high self-regard and, on the surface, it might look like all is well, but if their regard for themselves is conditional then it will be tenuous, fragile, unstable and associated with emotional instability and defensive social processes. With such people, it can feel like we are walking on eggshells when we are around them.

It is understandable that in this climate of educational pressure and consequent stress to perform in the modern workplace, people only see their value in terms of their success, wealth and status. It seems to me that we have created an economic and social system that is by its nature damaging to our psychological health. To achieve a positive view of ourselves most of us inevitably step into the competitive rat race. And equally inevitably, most people fail to achieve the very heights of success, wealth and status needed to feel positive about themselves, and many succumb to problems of anxiety and depression because of their failure.

Many, who go to psychotherapy, arrive with one problem that they want to explore, but it quickly turns out that what is troubling them is something that lies behind that problem. Take Lisa, for example. She was very successful in her career, but her life was also falling apart. At first, she thought her problem was her drinking, but she came to understand that her drinking was her way of managing the tension she felt within her.

'No wonder I was drinking; it was because of the contradictions. I was so good at my job; I could have sold anyone anything. I put so much into it, it's who I was. I was spending my life on calls and giving presentations. That's why it was so tiring. Afterwards I would go to the bar to unwind. People would tell me how good I was at my job, that I was such a "people person". I thought I loved it, because I was good at it, but actually I hated it and it was costing me my health. That's why I was drinking.

'It wasn't the drinking that was really the problem, that was just to take the pressure off; it was the job that was the problem, but I didn't realise. I was so worn out. It has taken me all this time to work out what I was doing. Now I know that just because I was good at it, and people told me I was excellent at it, it doesn't mean I should be doing it. It isn't me; it's taken me years to realise I don't have to feel bad about walking away.'

Lisa had felt stressed and anxious for many years. She needed to listen to her feelings, but she had covered them up with her drinking. Until she was able to realise that her acceptance of herself had been tied to others' expectations of her, not her own, she wasn't free to be who she was. It is a question that each of us should ask ourselves:

How much do we feel that we are pursuing a life in which we are able to be who we really are?

Alcohol use is one way to deal with the difficult emotions

stirred up by conditional self-regard. Research by the social psychologist Clayton Neighbours and his colleagues at North Dakota State University showed that those whose self-worth is contingent on others' expectations drank to regulate their emotions about themselves.[8] Alcohol can seem to help us deal, in the short term, with how we are feeling, but in the longer term it is more likely a wrecking ball in our lives. While Lisa managed to find her own inner voice in the end, not everyone does – and our conditional regard for ourselves can end up being destructive.

Another example is Frank, a businessman who had done well financially in developing products for the educational market – yet the success he had wasn't enough for him. He and his wife and three children were living in a modest-sized home in a picturesque village, surrounded by beautiful English countryside. In terms of materialistic success and having a comfortable lifestyle, theirs was far ahead of what most people have in England, never mind the world. But it wasn't enough. For Frank, surrounded by much larger and more expensive homes, some of which were tucked away behind imposing hedges and which housed some very famous and wealthy people, when compared with his well-dressed business acquaintances at his golf club, he wasn't good enough in his own eyes. Frank had decided at some point in his life that his value as a person rested almost entirely on his financial success. One year, after some bad business deals and subsequent psychiatric difficulties, Frank tried to take his own life. For someone like Frank, his threatened financial ruin meant that for him he was a person of no value or worth, and that was too hard for him to live with. I am not saying that wanting to be financially successful is a bad thing in its own right. There is nothing wrong with that, but what is damaging to a person is when it becomes their barometer to how they feel about themselves and their sense of self-worth, as was the case here.

For Frank, the road he was on started for him as a boy. His father was a successful businessman. Frank tells me that his father didn't seem to have much time for his children, but Frank longed for his father's approval. One of his earliest memories is of washing the neighbours' cars when he was about twelve years old and the pride he felt when he showed his father the money he had earned.

Children who experience unconditional regard from others when they are growing up develop unconditional regard for themselves, but those who experience conditional regard from others develop conditional self-regard, and they take this with them into adult life. In reading this chapter, you will probably have had your own memories come to mind of what messages you took on board as a child from the adults around you about what was and what was not important. Psychologists call this process 'introjection'. This is a common process of how children learn the rules, beliefs and values by which to evaluate themselves. That might seem obvious, but introjection is an unconscious process. Our introjections become so deeply embedded within us that we don't know they are introjections. We just believe that is who we are and what we think.

Each of us likes to think we have our own personality, likes and dislikes – it's who we are, we say. But think about it, what is left of us when we strip away all the introjections? Like the layers of an onion, as we peel the last layer away, there is nothing left. Who we think we are, all of it is just introjection.

Many of us grow up internalising the assumptions of those around us. In his commencement address to students at Stanford, Steve Jobs said, 'Your time is limited, so don't waste it living someone else's life. Don't be trapped by dogma – which is living with the results of other people's thinking. Don't let the noise of others' opinions drown out your own inner voice.' Helping people to dig down into the values they took on board as children is one of the tasks of psychotherapy. Carl Rogers famously developed a new type of therapy in which, in essence, a person transitions from conditional self-regard to unconditional self-regard. This occurs because of the unconditional positive regard provided to the client by the therapist. The therapist is someone who offers us unconditional acceptance, in a sense to make up for what we haven't had before in life and through that we learn to replace our conditional acceptance of ourselves with unconditional acceptance.

Imagine having the perfect therapist and that you are truly loved, accepted for who you are regardless of your faults and successes. Imagine feeling that, day after day, year after year, you are just accepted as you are. You have no need to prove yourself to anyone because you are enough already. Take a few moments to ponder what that might feel like. You would come to value yourself just as you are. In essence, therapy strips away all the introjections, it peels away the layers of the onion.

Sometimes, as a way of helping people to begin to explore the assumptions they have internalised, a therapist might instruct them:

Close your eyes, picture the house of your childhood, and imagine yourself as a child. You are standing at the front door. It opens. In your mind, walk into the home of your childhood.

They are then asked to imagine whoever was their main caregiver standing there. Often it would be the mother.

Your mother is standing there. She turns to face you and she says to you: 'Whatever you do in life, you must always ...' Finish that sentence in your mind. Just say whatever comes to mind.

Clients may then be asked to imagine a second caregiver speaking the same sentence. This helps people discover how early experiences with caregivers shaped their values. They often finish the 'You must always' sentence with instructions like 'work hard to succeed', 'be pretty', 'be clever', 'be nice to people', 'do as you are told', 'say your prayers', 'be clean', 'be a good boy', 'be a good girl' or 'hide your tears'. Whatever sentences you came up with may not be the actual words you ever heard spoken, or what was ever said to you, but these are the meanings you made at the time. As young people, susceptible to the influences of the adults around us, we work out what is supposed to matter, not just from the words we hear and the way we are treated, but also from the slightest gestures and looks.

In this way we grow up, developing beliefs about who we must be and what we must do if we are to be valued. We develop conditional self-regard – 'I value myself insofar as I am successful, attractive, liked, obedient, religious, strong', or whatever. We become shackled to a list of 'oughts' and 'shoulds' that become, in a sense, our 'operating system'. Most of us have such beliefs, running deep down within us. Psychological growth requires us to have a different operating system, one in which we are governed instead by unconditional beliefs. Instead of thinking, for example, 'If I don't do well in my career, I'm worthless', we would say to ourselves: 'I'd like to do well in my career, but no matter how that goes I will value myself regardless.' Or instead of thinking, 'I can only like myself if I'm the most attractive', think instead, 'I take care of my appearance, but whether I'm the most attractive person or not doesn't define who I am.'

Another question to ask is:

> Are there expectations or rules for living that you carry around in your head that were perhaps useful at one point in your life but are now out of date?

For Frank, his inability to contend with his conditional self-regard was turned inward in a destructive way. For others, the feelings might have a more outward expression, as those pent-up feelings get released in anger or violence. As a therapist I listen to people lashing out at others, spraying blame around them, all to protect their own fragile sense of self. Some people go through life building their defences in exactly this way until they truly believe their own excuses. The bars of our prison cell are often invisible to us such that we don't understand the prison we are in, how restricted our thoughts are and how we fail to question ourselves.

Only by accepting ourselves are we able to drop the defences that keep us stuck and be more realistic about ourselves. For example, an ingenious study by John Chamberlain and David Haaga at the American University in Washington, had participants give a short speech to others.[9] Afterwards, they were asked to rate how good they thought their speech was. It was found that those higher on unconditional self-acceptance gave themselves more accurate ratings. When given negative feedback which they were led to think was from the observers, they were also less likely to denigrate the observers. In sum, when we truly accept ourselves, we become less defensive, more realistic and more accepting of others.

When we are governed by introjected values, beliefs and expectations, and trying to maintain a self-regard that is conditional on meeting these values, beliefs and expectations, we are not free to be ourselves. Being free to be yourself does not mean anything goes. I don't mean that we should ignore the rules of society and social conventions and just do whatever we like whenever we like. Of course not. But I am saying that it is psychologically healthy to become aware of the layers that make up your sense of who you are and strip away those layers that are no longer helpful to you. If your aim in life is to please other people, especially if you don't know it, the fact is you will always feel like you are a disappointment and that you are the subject of scorn, ridicule and criticism. That is the life experience of many people who come to therapy, a constant sense of being a disappointment, of not being enough, of being a failure, always feeling criticism of who they are and what they do.

I do know that criticism can't be avoided. If you do something, someone somewhere probably won't like it. By doing something, you make yourself a target for other people's ridicule, anger, resentment or loathing. You can't avoid criticism from other people unless you make yourself invisible. That leads some people to shrink inside themselves, to try to disappear, to hide from others so that there is nothing left of them to criticise. We even hold how we feel in our bodies, hunched over and looking down at the floor to hide ourselves. But while that is one way to cope, it is a path to self-destruction. There will always be the possibility of criticism of anything you do, you can't change that, but what you can change is how you respond.

You can respond to criticism differently when those feelings of conditional regard for yourself are peeled away and replaced with self-acceptance. For many of us, however, to become more unconditionally accepting of ourselves requires a lot of unlearning. We must now learn to look within ourselves rather than outside ourselves. There is a quote attributed to the Buddha: 'As solid rock remains unmoved by the wind, so the wise remain unmoved by blame and praise.'

Imagine if you truly valued yourself just for who you are, not for who you are in the eyes of others. Take five minutes to try the following exercise.

- Take a breath in through your nose for the count of 7, hold it for 4.
- Expel it through your mouth for 9.
- On the 'in' breath, I want to you visualise a sign lit up in neon that says 'I am a person of worth just as I am'.
- On the 'out' breath, visualise another sign, that says 'I don't have to be a people pleaser.'

See how you feel after trying it for a few minutes.

Once you have got used to the exercise, feel free to play with it and modify it to suit you. You might want to imagine different sayings on the neon signs. I gave an example of a statement for the out breath, but you might also find it useful to start the exercise with the in breath, and then just see whatever comes to mind for the out breath. If you let whatever images or words come to mind, you may be surprised at what comes up. You may find words or images that remind you of something you hadn't thought of for a long time. When you find yourself surprised by an image or a word, stop the exercise for a few minutes and use that time to reflect on what it means for you. As a way of unlocking memories and beginning to peel away the layers of the onion, this exercise can be very helpful.

Think about the different life you could lead if you felt free to be yourself. Ask yourself, are there hopes, dreams or aspirations that you have and that are important to you, but you keep putting to one side? Sometimes change seems too difficult. Only when we can accept ourselves, just as we are, are we able to change. In these ways, unless we can have unconditional self-regard, we will never feel free to be ourselves, as we look to others for vindication, approval and validation.

The quote from Carl Rogers with which I opened this chapter captures the essential paradox at the heart of changing our lives: with self-acceptance we don't seek to change who we are, but that's when it happens. With unconditional positive self-regard comes the ability to trust what our feelings tell us, to know what decisions are right or wrong for us, and to take responsibility for our choices. The ability that comes naturally to us when we can accept ourselves unconditionally is that we look within ourselves for answers. We learn to trust our gut, our instincts and intuition, and to understand the wisdom of what our emotions are telling us. It is about being able to form our own judgements about what we like and dislike and evaluate information for ourselves without always having to look to others. If offered a new job, or thinking about any major life decision, we may ask others what they think to get their perspectives, but we will evaluate for ourselves all the evidence available to us and what our feelings tell us.

The self-accepting person is guided by their own internal standards and values, not the external standards of others, takes responsibility for their actions, observes what others say about them objectively, is honest with themselves about their motivations and abilities, respects themselves as a human being worthy of being loved. In short, with self-acceptance comes personal power, the topic of the next chapter.

3

Power Brokers

*'The most common way people
give up their power is by thinking
they don't have any.'*

I love this quote from the novelist Alice Walker. It conveys such an important truth: we are ultimately the authors of our own lives, yet too often we let others dictate the direction and shape they take, thus giving up our power. Most people don't choose to do this though, or even realise they have done it. A lot of the psychology on the topic of power is about power over others, but this chapter deals with personal power, the power we have over ourselves – the power to know how we feel and think, to make our own decisions about what matters and what direction to go in and to have the resources within us to move forward.

The subtle nature of this process by which we give up our personal power is illustrated in one of my favourite movies, *The Wizard of Oz*. In it, Dorothy, the Tin Man, the Lion and the Scarecrow defeat the Wicked Witch and return to the Emerald City. The Great Wizard has promised to grant their wishes if they defeat the witch. Dorothy hopes to return home to Kansas, the Tin Man desires a heart, the Lion courage and the Scarecrow brains. Cowering before the booming voice of the Wizard, Dorothy and her chums ask him to fulfil his promise. But, by accident, the curtain falls away. The Wizard is revealed as a small, old man speaking into a megaphone and pulling frantically at levers. It is all smoke and mirrors. The Wizard realises that his deception has been revealed. 'I'm not a bad man, just a bad wizard', he says. But Dorothy's chums insist he keeps his promise.

The Wizard presents the Tin Man with a clock, the Lion with medals and the Scarecrow with a certificate. He is a wise man, for the Wizard knows that the human qualities of heart, courage and brains cannot be given. As such, the Wizard offers his gifts allegorically. In giving these gifts he knows that, through their trials and tribulations, what Dorothy's companions are seeking has always been within them. During their adventures, the Tin Man has admirably shown his heart, the Lion his bravery and the Scarecrow his brains. Not realising that the gifts are only symbols – the ticking of the clock representing the heart the Tin Man so wished for, the medals representing the valour that the lion craved and the certificate showing the achievement of learning that the Scarecrow sought – and not the things themselves, Dorothy's chums dance with delight, as if they have actually been given these gifts of heart, courage and brains. They look to the Wizard rather than within themselves for what they need. *The Wizard of Oz*, for me, illustrates the importance of learning to trust our guts, our instincts and our own minds. It is about being able to form our own judgements about what we like and dislike and evaluating information for ourselves, without always having to look to others.

In psychology this is called the 'locus of evaluation' and it is vital to our personal power.[1] Some of us have an *internal* locus of evaluation, where we look within ourselves for answers; others of us, an *external* locus of evaluation, where we look outside ourselves for the answers.

Those who look outwardly are, in a metaphorical sense, always tugging at others' sleeves to get their guidance, to have someone else tell them what to do next or reassure them in some way that they are OK. As a therapist, it is easy to spot whether a person has an internal or an external locus of evaluation. Those with an external locus look to me for the answers, but those with an internal locus talk with me in a very different way. They aren't looking for me to tell them what to do or how to think, but using me in the opposite way, as a sounding board, to hear themselves more clearly. It is the same in the classroom. Those students with a more external locus of evaluation wait to be told which book to read next, but those with an internal locus of evaluation come to class having already read the book. The latter also tend to have what's referred to as an internal 'locus of control'.

Locus of control has been one of the most heavily studied concepts in psychology over the past fifty years. It describes how people generally have an internal or an external expectation about the source of control in their lives. The term was introduced in 1966 by the psychologist Julian Rotter at the University of Connecticut, in what has become one of the most cited research psychology papers of all time.[2] Rotter's idea was that people differ in their expectancies of control in their lives. Some people have what he called an *internal* locus of control, whereas others have an *external* locus of control. To assess the degree to which people had one or the other, Rotter presented his subjects with a list of forced choice statements. For example, one choice on his questionnaire asked people to choose between two statements about misfortune in life.

1. Many of the unhappy things in people's lives are partly due to bad luck.

or

2. People's misfortunes result from the mistakes
   they make.

Those agreeing with the first statement are more likely to be classified as having an external locus of control, whereas those who agree with the second have an internal one. This gives us a sense of whether we see our personal lives as within our control or not. So, how about this next choice between two statements about success in life?

1. Becoming a success is a matter of hard work; luck
   has little or nothing to do with it.

or

2. Getting a good job depends mainly on being in the
   right place at the right time.

This time, those who agree with the first statement are more likely to be classified as having an internal locus of control, whereas those who agree with the second have an external one. Other statements in Rotter's questionnaire were about wider political events in the world. For example, how would you choose between these next two statements about war:

1. One of the major reasons why we have wars is
    because people don't take enough interest in politics.

or

2. There will always be wars, no matter how hard
    people try to prevent them.

In this instance, if you had agreed with the first statement, you would be classified as having an internal locus of
control, with the second, an external locus.

How about the following two statements about politics?

1. With enough effort we can wipe out political
    corruption.

or

2. It is difficult for people to have much control over
    the things politicians do in office.

Those who agree with the first statement are more
likely to be classified as having an internal locus of control,
whereas those who agree with the second, an external locus.

Other statements were about human relationships.
For example, what about the reasons for how people
gain respect?

1. In the long run, people get the respect they
   deserve in this world.

or

2. Unfortunately, an individual's worth often passes
   unrecognised no matter how hard they try.

Here, agreement with the first statement indicates an internal locus of control and agreement with the second, an external locus of control.

If you ask yourself these questions, your responses will give you some clue about your own sense of control in life, and whether if you were to take the full test devised by Rotter you would be classified as having an internal or external locus of control.

Since Rotter published his groundbreaking work, many other psychologists have developed and elaborated on his original idea, developing more sophisticated tests to assess our sense of control over life. Rotter's questionnaire assumed that there was a general sense of control that people had that could be classified along a continuum of internal to external, and while at a broad level this remains most likely true, many other researchers have since put a microscope on to the fine detail. It may be for instance that people's locus of control differs depending on whether they are talking about personal events, interpersonal events, or political events. You may have felt that yourself when answering the questions above. It may also be that it is too simple to think about an external locus of control as just one thing – in one important observation, Hanna Levenson at Texas A&M University proposed that externality could be broken down into two types, the first was believing in chance, the second, that powerful others influence things.[3]

Over the years, a vast literature has developed on the role locus of control has in our lives and how it relates to our well-being. Having an internal locus of control is related to better health because the more we feel in control of our lives, the more we will do something to prevent ourselves getting ill and take actions that may be helpful to us when we are, in fact, ill. Indeed, some researchers have gone so far as to study what they call 'health locus of control', distinguishing people who believe that health is determined by their own behaviour, those that feel it is all down to chance or luck and those who see powerful others as making the difference.

Kenneth Wallston of Vanderbilt University and his colleagues, Barbara Wallston and Robert DeVellis are among the pioneers in this field. Wallston and DeVellis developed a questionnaire in 1978 to assess different beliefs about health which is still widely used by psychologists.[4] To give you an example, read each of the following three statements and think about which one you most agree with.

1. If I get sick, it is my own behaviour which
    determines how soon I will get well again.
2. Having regular contact with my physician is the
    best way for me to avoid illness.
3. No matter what I do, if I am going to get sick, I
    will get sick.

The answer you give tells you whether you are inclined to see yourself as in control, whether it is down to powerful others or just a matter of chance.

Some years later, Kenneth Wallston and other colleagues explored belief in God as another form of external control in patients with either rheumatic diseases, rheumatoid arthritis or systemic sclerosis.[5] Those who agreed with statements such as *'Whatever happens to me is God's will'* did not adjust as well to their disease when compared to those who disagreed and had a more internal locus of control. While it makes sense that in some circumstances, such beliefs may lead people to take less responsibility for their actions, in other circumstances could a belief in God be helpful? Inevitably, there is a relationship between our beliefs about religion and our beliefs about control, but what that relationship looks like is not straightforward and will be different for different people. In some circumstances, a reliance on God may improve one's sense of internal control, for example, in giving us strength to cope with a situation or a sense that God is working to help us in the best way.[6]

Digging down deeper into the idea of locus of control, we can also think about how it affects the various other domains in our lives and whether or not we can achieve our goals to do with our relationships or our work life and careers. Inevitably, the more one has an internal locus of control, the more one can achieve personal goals. This is because those with an internal locus tend also to have a *sense of agency*. This is vital for achieving our goals, regulating our emotions and coping with challenging situations. Not only must we know what to do, we must be able to orchestrate the events in our lives.

Those who are more able to do this are said to have high *self-efficacy*. A concept introduced in 1977 by the renowned Stanford psychologist Albert Bandura,[7] self-efficacy refers to a person's belief in their ability to do what is necessary to produce the outcome they want.

Locus of control and self-efficacy seem like closely related ideas, but there is a subtle difference. Someone with an external locus of control will inevitably have low self-efficacy because they do not see that they can produce the outcome. Someone with an internal locus of control will see that they can produce the outcome, so it is only possible to have self-efficacy if you have an internal locus of control. But an internal locus of control doesn't necessarily mean a person will have high self-efficacy. For example, someone may know that they have the skills for a job and that they need to submit an application – they have an internal locus of control – but they fail to do it, because of poor time management skills – so, they have low self-efficacy.

The following are some questions that will help you think about how you stand on this dimension of self-efficacy.

1. Are you the sort of person who, when you make plans, are certain that you can make them work?
2. Do you keep trying at a task until it is achieved?
3. Do you feel capable of dealing with whatever problems arise in your life?

A 'yes' to these questions would suggest that you are someone with a high degree of self-efficacy.

I hope reading the above will have given you a sense of your own standing on these two important dimensions of locus of control and self-efficacy, and allow some opportunity for reflection on which aspects are strongest and most well-developed within you, and which are most in need of building up. Those with personal power can evaluate their experiences without looking to others, have a realistic sense of control over their lives and see tasks as something to be mastered and challenges to be overcome.

It is important that we can find our sense of personal power, especially when we are at our lowest. A sense of powerlessness can be detrimental both to our well-being and our physical health. Melvin Seeman and Susan Lewis, sociologists at the University of California,[8] studied adults over a period of ten years, concluding that a sense of powerlessness was related to a deterioration in health and even increased mortality over that time.

Amanda, for example, grew up in a rural village in Scotland, with strict religious and authoritarian parents, so right from her early years she learned that she had little control and self-efficacy as she was bound by sets of external rules and standards. She struggled to find her own direction in the world but eventually took a degree in business studies, for no other reason than she thought it would be a good qualification to help her to find a job. On finishing university, her first job was with the first company that offered her a position, one that she had applied for simply because they were looking for people with a business degree. She did well, moving into a more senior position specialising in marketing, after five years. A few years later, she was approached by another organisation, interested in her as a marketing specialist, to head up a new project line. It was in this new role that everything seemed to go wrong for her, and after two years she was dismissed.

This proved to be the turning point for Amanda. At

first, in the days after her dismissal, she struggled to get out of bed in the mornings. Her friends and family were worried about her. But during this time, something else was going on: she began to think about how, in her career and her life, she had gone from one thing to the next, without any sense of direction of her own choosing, and always putting her job first at the expense of herself. She was the first in and the last to leave, always trying to please her line manager.

At the end of one of our sessions, a few months later, Amanda turned to me with a look of determination on her face, 'I did everything in that job to please them, and in the end, they couldn't care about me. Never again.' In that moment, as I watched Amanda, she seemed to take back her personal power. She realised that she had given up her power previously. Over the next sessions with me, she explored what she wanted to achieve and experience in life for herself, something that she felt she had never done before. When she eventually found a new job, one that involved promoting awareness of environmental issues, it was something that she was genuinely interested in, and which she was able to approach with a different attitude, taking control of her choices.

If we are in a relationship that we don't want to be in, we can leave it and seek a new relationship. If we are in a job that we dislike, we can seek a new job. This might sound obvious, but the reality is that a lot of people live their life as if these statements weren't true. That they have no choice. We fail to understand how our perceptions of personal power are not always realistic appraisals. Generally, research shows that those with a greater sense of internal locus of control in life and a stronger sense of self-efficacy are happier,[9] and these qualities that give us agency and autonomy help us skilfully navigate life. For most people the problem is that they underestimate themselves in these respects.

If we underestimate our personal power, it can be to our detriment, not just personally but to the shape and direction the world takes. Below are pairs of statements. Choose the one statement from each pair that you most strongly believe to be true.

a. The world is run by the few people in power, and there is not much the ordinary person can do about it.

b. The ordinary person can have an influence on government decisions.

a. There is very little we can do to bring about a permanent world peace.

b. A lasting world peace can be achieved by those of us who work towards it.

a. More and more, I feel helpless in the face of what's happening in the world today.
b. I sometimes feel personally to blame for the sad state of affairs in our government.

These questions seem so relevant to people's lives today that you may be surprised to know that they were originally published in 1964 in the powerlessness questionnaire developed by Melvin Seeman.[10] If you answered 'a' to the three pairs of statements above, it is likely you feel a high degree of powerlessness, at least with the political events in the world.

Of course, there are times when one's sense of powerlessness simply reflects the reality of a situation. I am not advocating some kind of naive optimism about our influence, but what I am saying is that our perception of reality and our sense of powerlessness are intertwined. When we feel powerless, we may think that is the reality even when it isn't.

Research shows that feeling powerless affects how people see the world. Eun Hee Lee and Simone Schnall at the University of Cambridge's Department of Psychology carried out experiments in which volunteers were surveyed about their sense of power, using a questionnaire like the one described above, then asked to lift boxes of varying weights and guess how heavy they were.[11] Those who felt more powerless perceived the weight of the boxes as much heavier than those who felt more powerful.

In a further twist to the experiment, they asked participants to sit in either an expansive, domineering position – with one elbow on the arm of their chair and the other on the desk next to them – or a more constricting one, with hands tucked under thighs and shoulders dropped. Those who sat in the more powerful pose gave more accurate estimates of the weight, while those in the submissive condition continued to imagine heavier weight. Another twist was to ask participants to recall an experience in which they had felt either powerful or powerless, and then estimate the weights of various boxes. Those who focused on the powerful incident became more accurate at guessing the weight, while those recalling a powerless situation continually overestimated the heaviness of the boxes.

Having a sense of personal power therefore is important in shaping the sort of lives that we lead, our relationships, careers and the things that matter to us. In a now classic experiment, published in the *Journal of Personality and Social Psychology*, which illustrated just how true this is, the social psychologist Adam Galinsky and his colleagues found that participants who felt powerless were less likely to turn off a fan when left in a chilly room than those who felt powerful.[12] If this is what happens in a controlled psychology experiment, imagine the different ways in which the powerless and the powerful approach the challenges of real life.

Too often, we act like tin men, scarecrows and cowardly

lions by giving our power away to others and, in a metaphorical sense, overestimating the heaviness of the boxes we carry and not turning off the fan when we are cold. No one knows this better than politicians, marketers, advertisers, religious leaders and all those who have a vested interest in persuading us to their causes. To these people, we easily and unquestioningly give our power away.

It is in the interests of many individuals and organisations to let us think that the boxes we carry are heavier than they are and that the switch to the fan is only for their use. We also know from social psychology experiments over the past sixty years just how easily people can be swayed to the causes of others. Solomon Asch, in the 1950s, showed how some people were prone to conformity and Stanley Milgram, in the 1960s, showed that others have a tendency towards obedience when there is an authority figure.

In Asch's famous experiment, he had people come into his laboratory at Swarthmore College, Pennsylvania. They sat around a table and he asked them in turn to estimate the length of different lines presented to them on a series of cards. He found that many people's answers were influenced by the answers of those who went before them. And when those who went before were secretly working with Asch and deliberately gave the wrong answers, people were still inclined to go along with that answer. It was like the desire to conform was so strong that people mistrusted what they were seeing with their own eyes and lost confidence in themselves.

In Milgram's experiment, participants were invited to take part in a study at Yale University that involved them giving electric shocks to other people as part of an investigation into learning. But the point of the experiment wasn't really about learning, but about obedience. Milgram wanted to find out how much people would increase the voltage of the electric shocks when he, as the person running the experiment and in a position of authority, asked them to. Of course, the situation was a set-up and the people receiving the electric shocks were only pretending to writhe in agony. But given that the participants didn't know that, it was a startling finding that many people obeyed his authority even when they thought they were being instructed to administer lethal shocks. Asch's and Milgram's studies, along with a host of others since, remind us of how we can be like billiard balls reacting to external forces.[13]

Our sense of personal power has its roots in our childhood. Often it is the people we are closest to, our family and friends, those who want us to be a certain way for them, that we give our power to and allow to sway our judgement. The interactions that are especially important are with the adults around us when we are young. We first develop a sense of our own personal power as young children through our interactions with others. As children, we may be encouraged by our parents and other adults to think for ourselves, make our own decisions, learn about taking responsibility for our actions and find our own direction in life. Parents like these foster personal power in their children.

On the other hand, parents who make their children's decisions for them, who do not provide them with the opportunities to learn about responsibility and who take complete control over the direction of their lives, thwart those children's developing sense of personal power. Those children with more controlling parents who dictate the direction of the child's life generally do their children a disservice, as they go on to be less confident, more uncertain and more likely to grow up lacking the sense of personal power. So used are they to giving away their power, they don't know they have it within them to do differently.

The patterns we learn when we are young, we take into adulthood. As adults we unwittingly hand our power over to friends, partners, employers, religious and political leaders, who may grab it for themselves and use it in their own interests. As a result, some people find themselves as adults in extreme coercive and controlling relationships because they lack the skills to identify these tendencies in others early enough to avoid getting involved with them. But while such extreme relationships are rare, very few of us escape some form of controlling relationships altogether. To a greater or lesser extent, all of us are tangled in a web of power relationships, each of us pushing and pulling for power, either to regain our own or to take it from others.

There are four broad types of power that others have over us. The first is 'reward power', when others have the ability to give us what we want. It may be a lover's affection, a friend's companionship, an employer's wage packet. We all live in a world in which we are interdependent, and we rely on others to meet our needs in life.

The second is 'coercive power', which is when others can potentially punish us and we are driven by fear. The threat of unemployment or wage reduction is a familiar use of coercive power. At times, that power can be used to manipulate us to act in ways that go against our better nature. We become puppets for others who pull our strings.

The third is 'referent power', when we are influenced to behave in ways that are similar to another person out of respect or admiration for them. Imagine a little boy who wants to be like his father. He tries to walk like him and adopts the same way he holds his head. But it's not only children who look up to their parents – throughout life we will be influenced by people we admire and, whether deliberately or not, will take on some of their qualities.

The fourth and final category is 'expert power', which is when we believe that someone else has greater knowledge than us and we allow ourselves to be influenced by their better judgement. Imagine there is an important decision to be made, but you are unsure what the right course of action is. The wise decision is to ask the opinion of someone who has more knowledge. We look to those people for their expertise.

All of these types of power have their place, but it is their misuse that is of concern. We need expert power, for example, but we need to know who the experts are and trust they have our best interests at heart. Those with power over us also fight among themselves, such as we have seen in recent years with those with expert power challenging those with coercive power, and those with coercive power downplaying the importance of those with expert power. If you watch the nightly news, observe the different forms of power in play and who you may be choosing to give your power away to.

We are surrounded by relationships that pull and push us in different directions, to induce us to perform in certain ways. It is important in life to learn about keeping boundaries, in our personal as well as working lives and to be able to say 'no' to requests that impinge on those boundaries. Otherwise, those relationships will drain us of our personal power. This is not to dismiss the very real experiences of powerlessness faced by many of us, and how hard it can be to maintain boundaries. In my experience, bullying and intimidation in workplaces is commonplace, such that many people often live in a constant state of anxiety about losing their jobs. These are power struggles that we can easily see being played out immediately around us every day. We can become so preoccupied with these that we take our eye off the bigger picture of how power is wielded in society.

Many of us now live only a few salary cheques away from destitution. In parts of the Western world, the average price of a home is now about ten times or more than the average salary, which makes just having somewhere to live a real problem for many people. This is not an issue though to the heads of some organisations who may have an annual salary of several million pounds or more, but rather to the employees who earn only a few pounds an hour. Such inequality in society is divisive and serves to further disempower people.

One of the things that often strikes me any time I take a flight is how much green space there is in the world and how little of it I am allowed on.[14] It makes me realise how almost all the land in the country I live in is closed to people like me. Some people own swathes of central London and other major cities, hundreds of thousands of acres of countryside, simply by the position of their birth, whereas others own virtually nothing and their day-to-day existence to feed and house themselves is a struggle. Most of us are much closer to the latter. Where we can go, how we can spend our time is restricted.

It seems to be getting harder for people to find and exercise their personal power. Powerlessness seems to me to be endemic in most groups in society. This is due to a number of factors, but chiefly it seems to be because of the rise of a more individualistic and consumer-focused society, that has detrimentally affected our lives. When I look around me today at the people I meet as clients or as students, they don't seem to me to be entirely free. Students seem weighed down with debt and worries about their futures. People seeking therapy seem to have problems that stem more from fear of losing their jobs, difficulties paying their bills, and being able to afford to look after their families. All of the forces I've been describing impact on our sense of control in life.

Since the 1960s, many researchers have studied people's sense of control in life. That allows us to look back over decades at research results to see if there have been any changes. This is what Jean Twenge and her colleagues did at the University of San Diego in 2004.[15] They examined the published research on people's sense of control, with the startling finding that since the 1960s, young people's locus of control has become more external. They suggested that this reflected changes in modern society in which people feel alienated and apathetic, and they commented that if such a trend continued it would be to the detriment of everyone. It does seem that personal power has been eroded, and it is increasingly important that we use the power that we still have to reclaim autonomy for ourselves.

Human beings need freedom to determine their own directions in life, but under such pressures from employers, paying bills, holding down secure employment, the fear of becoming destitute and struggling to feed and house ourselves and our families, the natural directions and urges for us to be freely ourselves become squashed. To simply survive, it becomes essential sometimes to put on a mask, to do what one ought to do and jump to meet other people's expectations of us.

Even on the best days, most of us must work in jobs that we would give up in an instant if we had the power to do so. If you are one of the many millions who must work to pay debts that keep you awake at night, who has fearful thoughts of losing their job, who worries about being able to afford a home to live in, it is you I am talking about. Your personal power is something that other people want to take from you. And so much has already been taken that you may not even notice.

The American commentator Gore Vidal summed it up when he said: 'The genius of our ruling class is that it has kept a majority of the people from ever questioning the inequity of a system where most people drudge along paying heavy taxes for which they get nothing in return.'

There is very little that a person can do by themselves to change the fact that they are born into an unequal society and that their personal power is restricted, but it is a mistake to think that you can do nothing. A bigger mistake is to accept the situation as it is – that is how we give away the power that we each as individuals do have. It is easy to assume inequalities and injustices are just how things are and not realise that they are up for discussion.

In any society that claims to be democratic, everything should be up for discussion about how we govern ourselves, the relationships between us and how things get done. It seems ever more important that we engage actively in helping to shape the future of our society. Earlier I mentioned Asch's famous studies on conformity with the dispiriting finding that many people will go along with what the majority says, despite the evidence of their own eyes, but what is less well known was that Asch also showed that at least as many people will stand their ground and show powers of independence. Likewise, in Milgram's study on obedience, around a fifth disobeyed his instructions, with more recent research suggesting that figure would be closer to one-third today.[16] There will always be those who do not easily succumb to social influence.

Take for example Lucille Times, the woman who inspired the Montgomery bus boycott in America in 1955. She first took action to boycott the city's bus company after the racial discrimination and intimidation she experienced from one of the drivers. She would drive to the bus stops in her own car offering waiting Black passengers free rides. 'You've got to fight ... ' she is reported to have said. 'You don't get nothing for free. I've been a fighter all of my days.'[17] Times' activism inspired others, including Rosa Parks, who, six months later, refused to move from the front section of a bus reserved for white people to the back, sparking the citywide boycott that eventually would lead to the end of racial segregation in transport. Such people as Lucille Times and Rosa Parks stand out among us, providing us with examples of people who take back their personal power. Each of us, too, has the potential to change the world around us. The powerful tend to act on the world, whereas the powerless react to the world. Instead of saying, for example, there is no point in voting, we should go to the polling stations and vote – and by doing so, we are taking responsibility for our choices and the direction society takes. We are taking back our power.

Simply put, human beings need a sense of personal power to determine their own directions in life if they are to flourish. Personal power is about understanding how power is given and taken in society and the role each of us plays in it. At one end of the spectrum, it is about deciding for yourself what shoes to wear in the morning and what to have for dinner that evening. At the other end, it is about taking the time to vote or to stand up for something you believe in. Under pressure, we become the powerless people who simply react to the world around us.

Interestingly, one way we may do that is by becoming more authoritarian. That is what Geoffrey Evans, at the London School of Economics, concluded in an intriguing study published in the *European Journal of Social Psychology* in the 1990s.[18] In a national survey, those with more authoritarian attitudes, such as beliefs in strong law and order policies, traditional values, capital punishment and restrictions on individual freedom, were found to have a greater sense of powerlessness. But the twist in Evans' study was that he also examined the effects of powerlessness in different social classes. Working-class people who felt powerless were more attracted to socialist views favouring ideas about economic redistribution. Middle-class people who felt powerless were more drawn to conservative views and opposed economic redistribution. Put simply, under economic threat, those with less want wealth redistributed, and those with more want to hold on to what they've got.

Who should hold the power over us is always the most fundamental political issue. When people experience insufficient liberation and freedom, they are likely to be dissatisfied with their lives and the more likely they are to want to find ways to increase their personal power. It's like thirst. People have a need to drink when water levels are depleted, but once they are satiated, they no longer benefit from drinking and their thirst subsides. I mentioned earlier the study showing a trend towards young people feeling increasingly powerless and not surprisingly, they are engaging less in formal politics, seen in a decline in voting and membership in political parties. But at the same time, perhaps we are now seeing a different form of engagement with greater use of online forums.[19]

Over the past several decades there has been a gradual shift in how people think of themselves, such that we have become consumers rather citizens. To take back power, it seems important that we think of ourselves less as consumers and more as active citizens. And perhaps this is now happening with the generation born since Twenge's study was conducted, feeling increasingly dissatisfied with their lives, and particularly aware that they will be the generation to experience the worst of climate change. Against this background, we have seen demonstrations and school strikes for climate protection all over the globe.

I am not advocating in this chapter that we should all become control freaks, simply that we understand how we give our power away and what difference it makes when we don't hand it over so readily to others. Understanding how others exploit us and gain power over us is vital in realising the personal power we have already within us. The story of *The Wizard of Oz* is also a good example if you are reading this chapter waiting for me to say something that will, like a miracle, restore your sense of personal power, because all I can do is drop the curtain. It is our own responsibility as adults to think about the power structures in our lives, how we give our power away to others and to make the decision that it is time to take it back. There is only so much control we have in life and to underestimate it would be just as unhelpful as to overestimate it, but it is also true that each day we are confronted by various decisions, and like anyone at a junction we either turn one way or the other.

I began this book by saying how our perspective was important in how we manage the challenges in our lives and how happy we are, but that is not to dismiss the real difficulties people experience. Until we are able to act on the world around us, however, we will always be its victims. Choosing our direction and moving forward wisely requires personal power. We live in a social world in which the successful exercise of our personal power requires us to be clear in our communication with others, to negotiate compromises when we must and overcome obstacles in our path. Personal power is not about pushing our way to the front, bullying others into submission or tricking people into giving us what we want. It is about having others willingly help us to achieve our goals and we, in turn, helping others to achieve theirs. No one when confronted by the question of what really matters to them in life decides that it is a good idea to have less personal power. But it is only when we choose to take control over our lives, to decide for ourselves what direction to take, that we can make the bigger decisions that lie in wait for us. Perhaps the biggest decision we can make is to lead a life that is true to ourselves. Research shows that with power, we feel more authentic and able to be consistent with our values and beliefs.[20]

Often, we run away from the power we actually have in fear of discovering ourselves, the responsibility seeming too great. The psychologist Abraham Maslow called this the 'Jonah complex', in reference to the biblical character Jonah who was asked by God to carry out a task, but in fear fled to sea. A storm followed Jonah and the other sailors who, superstitiously believing him to be responsible, cast him overboard where he was swallowed by a whale. After three days inside the whale and praying to God, he was regurgitated on to a beach where he now felt compelled to carry out his task. Like Jonah, we often run away from ourselves until we are pushed to our limits; only then can we find the strength to rise up and take our personal power. What we do with our personal power, the sort of lives we want to create for ourselves and others, and how we confront the challenge of learning about ourselves, will be topics I will return to in the following chapters.

4

Open-Minded

'Absorb what is useful, discard what is
not, add what is uniquely your own.'

Our survival depends upon our ability to change, learn and
grow, but to do this we must be flexible, be open-minded.
Those with an openness to learning about themselves, a
willingness to look for alternatives in their understandings
and the ability to change their minds when it matters, ultimately survive the best. They are the ones who weather the
storms of life, pick themselves up when times are hard and
succeed in their ambitions. As such, I was struck when I read
the quote at the beginning of this chapter by the renowned
martial artist Bruce Lee. For me, it conveyed succinctly this
essential wisdom of how to approach life, to be able to ask
ourselves in all situations, what can I learn?

I was surprised to discover that Bruce Lee was also something of a philosopher and that his ideas were remarkably similar to the ones I was writing about. One of the metaphors Lee famously used was in his advice to be like water, to be both soft and strong: soft in how water can easily absorb great force, but also strong in how it can wear down mountains over time. Water always finds its path, and this powerful metaphor conveys the idea of being able to go with the flow of nature, to how best conserve and use our energy by going with the natural bend of things.

This brought back memories for me as a boy one summer in the late 1970s when I was myself learning some martial arts and first encountered the idea of using my opponent's weight against them. I learned that you don't have to have more strength or height to overpower someone – all you need is to know how to use your opponent's own weight and momentum against them. As your opponent moves towards you, in that split second when they are off balance, with little effort, you can use their own weight against them to bring them down. That lesson stayed with me and, over the years, I have come to understand how it serves as a philosophy with which to approach life, to always go with the flow of nature, rather than railing against it. It sounds simple enough, but in practice it means to be open, fluid and always shifting when we have new experiences. In reality, our default position is usually the opposite. Instead of shifting in our views, opinions and beliefs, we tend to discard new information unless it fits with our prior expectations. Instead of becoming more agile and responsive, we become the heavy object that is too easily brought down by its own weight.

French philosopher Jean Paul Sartre wrote, 'A man is always a teller of tales, he lives surrounded by his stories and the stories of others, he sees everything that happens to him through them; and he tries to live his life as if he were recounting it.'[1] Instead of openness to learning from new experiences, we twist information to fit our view of the world and ourselves instead of truly learning. Our stories can end up as self-fulfilling prophecies. So, we need, as Bruce Lee observed, to first be able to absorb new information. In this chapter, I will talk through three psychological principles that explain what stops us being open-minded and how to change that in ourselves.

The first is our construction of reality. As we have seen in the previous chapters, we all form a view of ourselves early in our lives and that becomes who we think we are and the lens through which we understand what happens to us. We act as if how we perceive things is accurate and true. From childhood onwards, we create a picture of who we are, but at some point, the paint begins to dry and our picture becomes a finished portrait. This sense of ourselves becomes so important that we cling on to it, even when all evidence points the other way.

This takes us to the second principle: cognitive conservatism. People are slow to change and tend to perceive events in their lives in ways that maintain their view of themselves. As already mentioned, we twist information that we receive so that it fits what we already think. The more we encounter information that challenges or threatens us, the more we distort or deny it to defend ourselves and our version of reality. We do things like blame other people so that we don't have to face up to ourselves when we behave badly. To look reality in the eye is just too much, so we avoid it.

But there is a third principle: the desire for personal growth. That is always there, struggling to be heard against the background of our distorted view of reality. To me, reality is something along the lines of what the Buddhists mean – the true nature of things uncontaminated by the ideas we impose upon them. There is always a gap between reality and our perception. The tension between these principles of conservatism (to hold fast to our perceptions) and growth (to see reality as it is) can become unbearable, leading to an existential crisis. This is what happened to Amanda, who we met previously, and whose world came crashing down when she lost her job.

Amanda was shocked to be fired and felt she had been unfairly treated, as others who she thought were inferior to her had held on to their jobs. Throughout Amanda's life, things had gone well for her. She expected life to follow a simple formula: if you work hard, you will be rewarded, so this was a blow. Amanda fell into depression, and it wasn't until she began to challenge her beliefs that she realised the world was not as just and fair as she had wanted to think.

Rather than approaching the world defensively, avoiding challenges and threats to her sense of self, by distorting and denying her experiences to fit with her view of reality, Amanda now became more receptive to the world, more open to learning about herself and willing to take on new ideas and information. What she learned was to look at the world in a new way and that allowed her to accommodate rather than assimilate her experiences.

The terms 'assimilation' and 'accommodation' were used by the Swiss child psychologist Jean Piaget and it is to his theory I will now turn.[2] While Piaget's work was concerned with the ways in which children learn about the world more generally, the two processes he described also provide a way of understanding how we engage with the world. Piaget used the example of building blocks. Let's say a child learns to place one block on top of another. Playing happily, they build a tower of blocks and then suddenly encounter a magnet. Never having seen a magnet before, they think it is another building block and place it on top of the tower. This is *assimilation* – in this case, even though the magnet is different, the child treats it as if it were the same.

The child is engaged in a process by which they take

in new information about objects by trying out existing assumptions on new objects, but at that age children are open to learning and driven by curiosity. When the child accidentally discovers that this new building block attracts metal, they quickly learn and will begin to play with the magnet differently. This is *accommodation* – the process of modifying assumptions as a child encounters new information.

There will be periods when assimilation dominates and periods when accommodation comes to the fore, as the child finds an equilibrium between the two. Assimilation and accommodation are always in competition with each other when we have new experiences in life. Learning, according to Piaget, is a balancing act between assimilation and accommodation. Although Piaget was talking about how children learn, the same process comes into play when, as adults, we encounter any new information.

As adults, however, we can become closed to learning and driven not by curiosity but a need to keep things the same. It is as though we don't want to find out that the magnet is different from the other building blocks. There are several reasons why that might be. There can be a sense of safety and comfort in what we know. It can be important to us to be right – it can be hard to learn that things we believed and that have been important to us throughout our lives are wrong. Rather than admit to ourselves that we have made a mistake in the past and change our beliefs, we may become more entrenched in our beliefs, cling on to them ever more tightly and become defensive of them.

This is what we do daily: we encounter new information about ourselves and the world around us and we try to make it fit with how we already think. Assimilation is the process of trying to maintain our beliefs contrary to new information. An example is the anecdote about the man who thought he was dead. A friend, trying to convince him that he wasn't, asked, 'do dead men bleed?', 'No' said the man. So, the friend pricked his finger with a needle. The finger began to bleed. 'Ah,' said the man, 'dead men do bleed!'. This is an amusing example, but it accurately portrays how we become so caught up in our own assumptions that we interpret our experiences in a way that fits those assumptions, even when they are wrong and the truth is staring us in the face. In this context, Amanda, who believed that hard work pays off, was shocked when she was made unemployed. Her initial response was to blame herself. Had she not worked hard enough? In what way had she deserved this? She was trying to make sense of what had happened in terms of the beliefs she'd held about hard work paying off, in contrast to the reality of the situation – that sometimes things just happen.

Psychological growth arises through the process of accommodation, during which our assumptions are modified so that they fit the new information, rather than through the process of assimilation, which involves our effort to make the new information fit our assumptions. As we encounter new experiences, we need to get the balance right. Too much assimilation and we won't be able to adapt and respond to the ever-changing world; too much accommodation and we will feel forever lost, without a map of where we are and where we are going.

Since accommodation requires that we let go of our previous assumptions, it can be a difficult and deeply distressing process. Recognising the truth about ourselves can be the hardest first step. Watching other people go through it and come out the other end also makes for great television. If you have ever seen the television programme *Ramsay's Kitchen Nightmares*, where the chef Gordon Ramsey visits failing hotels and restaurants and turns them around, you will know what I am talking about. I remember one episode where Gordon visits an inn which is shabby in its decor and attracting few customers, but the owner seems oblivious to the failings of his establishment. Gordon first checks out the menu. He delivers the verdict: 'disgusting'. The owner is angry and confused about why Gordon is saying this. Gordon then checks out the rooms. The verdict is also not good. Under ultraviolet light, it shows that the bedclothes and carpets in the bedrooms are heavily stained. The owner storms off in a rage.

An hour later in television time, the hotel is redecorated,

the menu is streamlined, the owner is greeting guests as they stream in for the first time in years. As viewers sitting at home on our sofas watching the owner crying and hugging Gordon, telling him that he has saved his life, we ourselves might even be moved to tears, so profound are the changes in the owner's demeanour, their openness to learning and willingness to change.

The point is, quite simply, that the truth can be hard to hear, but that's how change comes about. I think a reason why such reality programmes are so compelling is that we see ourselves reflected in the owners of these failing restaurants and hotels. These stories tell us about ourselves, and how difficult and upsetting it is for us to take on board new information that runs counter to what we already think, especially when it challenges our perceptions of ourselves. After all, who are we if not the sum of our beliefs and assumptions?

In a sense, accommodation can represent the death of who we once were. The great physicist Albert Einstein is often quoted as having said, 'I must be willing to give up what I am in order to become what I will be.' Accepting this fact of life is the key to personal growth, but what a terrifying prospect it can seem; so, understandably, our initial reaction is often to try and hold on to our old assumptions instead of accommodating new information.

Psychologists have found that we are biased towards

assimilation and maintaining our worldviews. This phenomenon is the second principle of cognitive conservatism, which I mentioned earlier. We seek out information that fits with what we already think, and we try to ignore, deny and distort anything that does not. Think of the child who refuses to believe that Santa Claus doesn't exist, even after finding his presents hidden under his parents' bed. It might seem amusing to think of such a child, but not when we realise that even as adults, we can do similar mental gymnastics when it suits us.

We get locked into our own worldview. In general, most people are not interested in hearing others' views and opinions, at least not to the extent of really trying to see things from another's perspective, walking around in their shoes. Most people don't want to hear your view, but rather want to tell you theirs. Often people will simply want to hear what they already think, and they want you to think the same. In this way, they validate themselves and make sense of their stories about who they are and what they feel.

The truth is that most of us are deluded in the sense that we overrate our abilities, tell ourselves what we want to hear to boost our confidence or blame others in order to make ourselves feel better. In some ways, of course, this is what helps us get through the week and manage stressful jobs, difficult relationships and all the other challenges that life throws at us.

It is frightening to think about how fragile we are as human beings, and not surprisingly there is a great comfort in seeing the world as more safe and fair than it actually is. I've already mentioned Terror Management Theory, which says that people engage in thoughts and behaviours to protect themselves from their fear of death. A related idea is the 'just world hypothesis', a psychological principal that describes how people are motivated to believe that the world is a fair and orderly place where what happens to people generally is what they deserve.[3] Believing that bad things happen to bad people and good things happen to good people, brings a sense of relief and comfort to a person. In this sense, believing in a just world can have some benefits to us because it enables us to pursue long-range goals. It is only if we think that the world has some order and predictability that it makes sense to do something today for what it brings in years to come. Not surprisingly, it is hard to give up our belief in a just world and, despite evidence to the contrary, we often cling tightly on to it. While helpful to us in some ways, it can also be extremely dysfunctional and antisocial. One way to restore a sense of justice in the world is to blame the victim. Putting blame on others who are suffering from illness or oppression can help us feel more secure in our own lives. If someone's predicament is a result of their own actions, we can breathe a sigh of relief.

Blaming others for events in our own lives can also help us to maintain our own sense of self-worth. We can all think of people who cannot hear the truth about themselves and seem deaf to information that does not agree with their worldview. Think of your colleagues at work who do not admit their responsibility when things go wrong. Often, they lash out at others, defending their fragile sense of self. To some degree, we all do this, at least some of the time. It's how we are built. It can be hard to think about our own defensive processes. The more defensive we are, the less likely we are to recognise that we are being defensive. But other people can see it in us if they pay attention. If other people were asked about you, would they say any of the following were true?

- You ignore certain things as if they didn't exist.
- You don't show your feelings.
- You act quickly without thinking.
- You think it is clever to criticise others.
- You eat to make yourself feel better.
- You think other people mistreat you.
- You are never satisfied.
- You get ill when things don't go right for you.
- You always justify yourself even when you are in the wrong.

These are the sort of things people do to help them alleviate feelings of stress. Most of us do some of these some of the time, but when these behaviours become the typical pattern, and describe how a person generally reacts to events in their life, it is likely that person has what might be thought of as a defensive personality style.[4]

What I have observed is how cognitive conservatism in people can be so damaging, because they fail to realise the opportunities for learning about themselves and go through life repeating the same mistakes. You might have heard the phrase that the universe will keep sending us the same lesson until we learn it. Well, that's true, although you don't need to invoke anything spiritual or supernatural for it to be true. Whatever the reason might be that we make mistakes, we will make the same mistake time and again, until we learn what it is we are doing. Someone who is driven by greed, will approach life greedily. Someone who is driven by fear, will approach life fearfully. Someone who is impatient, will approach life without patience. Each will make mistakes characterised by their greed, fear, or impatience.

When we are driven by a rigid way of thinking and feeling that we apply to all situations regardless, we end up making assumptions. Assumptions stop us seeing the world as it is, as we fail to question, look closely and see things from different angles. We assume we know what someone will say, so we don't ask. We assume how much it costs, so we don't offer.

If you have never fallen into this trap in some way yourself, you are unusual – in fact, you probably have but don't yet realise it. Most of us can look back on our lives and see how making assumptions has been to our detriment in the past. Whatever it is that drives a person will continue to do so until they work it out for themselves and allow themselves to approach life without greed, fear, impatience or whatever it might be, and with an open and questioning mind. The universe will of course then send the next set of lessons to learn. Living is about learning, and learning is what is meant by personal growth.

Bruce Lee, whose words began this chapter, also talked about discarding what is not useful. As humans, we are conservative when it comes to revising our mental models. We try to interpret new experiences within existing mental models. We continue to hold on to our existing models and to assimilate, rather than to accommodate new information. The challenge is ultimately to understand ourselves well enough to know what parts of ourselves we are defending, and to be able to approach life with an open mind, always willing to admit we were wrong, and eager to find new and more realistic ways to view ourselves and the world. The key here is that we want to be as realistic about ourselves and the world as possible.

I talked in the previous chapters about how children pick up messages from those around them about what is important, and how these messages take deep root, becoming the driving influence in the person's life. An example is Aniyah who recalls how, when she was young, she picked up the message from her parents, both of whom were teachers, that it was important to do well at school from an early age. She remembers that she always said that she herself wanted to be a teacher. Looking back, she says that her own inclinations were towards artistic and creative work, but she felt under pressure from her parents and from the advice at school to study more scientific subjects, going on to study biological sciences at university.

Years later, Aniyah had become a teacher in a successful school and was thought to be on her way to becoming a head teacher. The idea that she wanted to be a teacher was so deeply internalised in her psyche that she just accepted it as part of herself, but actually she was tired a lot of the time, didn't enjoy her work and found the long hours in the classroom stressful. Despite a sense of discomfort that somehow she was on the wrong track in life, she wasn't listening to herself. If you asked her, she would have told you that she was doing what she had always wanted. That is, until she was diagnosed with breast cancer. The diagnosis and the subsequent months of treatment were a wake-up call for Aniyah, who then began to listen more closely to herself and through that came to realise that deep inside, the track she was on was not her own; instead she had internalised as a young girl the messages from her parents about what was important.

Her treatment was successful, and Aniyah was now determined to change the track of life that she was on. She remembered the joy she had once achieved through her drawing and artwork as a child, and she began thinking about how to change the course of her life to meet her need to express herself more creatively and to find ways of living that seemed truer to who she felt she was, rather than who she had become. It involved some careful financial restructuring of her life but after going back to college, she now works as an artist and illustrator for children's books and is thinking of becoming an art therapist as a next step in her journey of personal growth.

Returning to the quote which opened this chapter, Bruce Lee's daughter, Shannon, in her biography of her father, describes how he would encourage people to seek understanding by asking themselves: 'Was I paying attention? Did I ask all questions? Did I find out the answers? Was I listening? Do I understand what happened? Was I open to the whole experience?'[5]

When we genuinely begin to ask ourselves such questions and challenge ourselves, we are no longer willing to put on a facade. We become more open about who we are, what we think and how we are feeling. No longer driven by 'oughts', we begin to live life as we see it. No longer willing to do what others expect of us, we move towards greater self-direction. No longer content with the old certainties, we begin to embrace the richness of life. We can choose to see our lives as an ever-changing adventure, in which there is always something new to learn about ourselves. We can choose to open our eyes to the complexities of the world and become more open to new experiences, seeking to learn, change and enjoy the challenges ahead. In doing all this, we will become more accepting of others and more trusting of ourselves, especially of our inner emotional lives.

Lisa, who we met earlier, had felt stressed and anxious for many years. She needed to listen to those feelings, but she had covered them up with her drinking. Until she was able to realise that her acceptance of herself was tied to others' expectations, she wasn't free to be who she was. Like many of us, Lisa was scared of her feelings. As a child she learned that angry or sad feelings were unacceptable, that it wasn't OK to disagree with people and that asking for things for herself was selfish, and to do any of these things was something to be ashamed of. It was just not what a good girl was like. She learned to suppress her feelings. 'I felt that life was pointless, like I was just waiting for death all the time. I was always tired, bored, and life wasn't for me.'

What Lisa needed to learn was that her feelings weren't the problem, the issue was how she dealt with them. It is impossible to fully push feelings down – they ultimately find a way out, often leaking out in very destructive ways. If we want to understand ourselves, we need to know which of our feelings are those we don't allow ourselves to experience and learn to reconnect with them in healthy ways. Our feelings exist to guide us through life. They are signposts showing us what we want and what we don't want so we can find our directions in life.

We need to become able to listen to what our feelings tell us. For some people this is extremely hard. They struggle to identify what they are feeling. Commonly, those who struggle the most to identify their emotions will say that they feel tired, so hard is it for them to identify and get in touch with their own emotions. Others might say they are feeling out of sorts or recognise that they are experiencing meaningful and upsetting feelings, but struggle to differentiate between different emotions of, for example, anger and sadness. They aren't sure really what they are feeling. Some might get confused and express themselves angrily but on exploration we find that it is actually sadness they are experiencing. Others might do the opposite and exhibit sadness when really it is anger that they are feeling.

Our emotions are such a powerful and helpful guide to us in life. It is important that we get better at knowing what we are feeling so we can make better decisions. For Lisa, by pushing her feelings away, she was detracting from her ability to experience the richness of life. It is a mistake to think of upsetting emotions simply as something bad to get rid of, as they are always telling us something about ourselves, the meaning and values we attach to events in our lives, and how to move forward.

Emotions have purpose. Anxiety keeps us on the lookout for what could go wrong. Sadness makes us reassess a situation. Anger prompts us to assert ourselves. But people often have an emotion that is more familiar or comfortable for them, and a bit like the adage that if you only have a hammer then everything is a nail, you tend to see the world only through the lens of that emotion. You are always on edge looking for danger, always ruminating over situations, or always up for a fight. It is exhausting, and not a productive way to be in the world. We need to be able to feel the range of emotions and use the benefits of each. Our feelings are what guide us, alongside our intellect. With both working together we can make the best decisions for ourselves. Returning again to Steve Jobs, his final advice at his Stanford address was: 'Most importantly, have the courage to follow your heart and intuition. They somehow already know what you truly want to become.'

We need to be at one with our emotional life. One place to start is to think about your attitudes towards emotional expression and work towards developing a more positive understanding of emotions and their expression.

- Are you the sort of person who thinks getting emotional is a sign of weakness?
- When upset, do you bottle up your feelings?
- Do you feel that you ought not to burden other people with your problems?
- Do you worry about the consequences of expressing your emotions, for example, that others will reject you, think less of you, or even that you will harm others?

People who have a negative attitude towards emotional expression typically answer these questions in the affirmative.[6] Such people also tend to be less open to experience and to score higher on measures of depression and anxiety and are, not surprisingly, less likely to seek social support from others when they are faced with difficulties and in need of help. A person's attitude towards emotional expression is thought to be linked to a variety of problems; those with a more negative attitude are more vulnerable to the effects of stress.[7]

The belief that one should not express emotions might result from having high levels of social anxiety, a need to appear perfect, or unhealthy beliefs regarding defectiveness, feelings of shame and a fear of abandonment. That said, undoubtedly, there will be many occasions in life when it is best to keep your feelings to yourself, but the wise person does their best to work out what to do in each situation. What

I'm talking about here is when people give themselves a blanket ban on emotional expression. If that sounds like you, then trying to find a way to develop a more positive and explorative attitude towards your emotions is likely to be helpful.

Alongside that, if we can be less defensive and rigid in our way of being, we can move towards a greater openness to our experiences in life, such that we would agree with such statements as the following:

- Life is an adventure and I enjoy the unknown.
- I enjoy learning new things about myself, others and the world.
- I see life as a journey and I appreciate that things will change.
- I feel I'm constantly learning new things about myself, other people, and the world.

What I am describing is an increasing fluidity as people come to open themselves to honest self-reflection and a willingness to change. Lisa had tried talking to therapists before who had offered her techniques to help her sleep better, ways of reducing her alcohol intake and methods for dealing with stress. All had seemed to help for a while, but in the long run her problems were piling up; such changes in her life were superficial and short-lasting, until Lisa also became willing to change herself.

But at the same time as becoming more open to change in themselves, people become more solid in themselves. Such people can hold these two positions, being aware of themselves and able to change and grow as the evidence of their senses takes them, but also able to stand resolutely to uphold their values and beliefs at other times. A person who is firm but lacks fluidity is rigid, and the stresses of constantly defending their view of themselves will ultimately lead to fractures that will be expressed in various ways such as anger, hostility, depression and low self-worth. On the other hand, fluidity without firmness will lead a person to feel confused about who they are and lost in what to think.

Earlier I talked about some of the difficulties in communication that arise between people when they are locked into their own worldviews, but we become more fluid and flexible in our thinking and feeling, our communication styles will change, as we won't want to get sucked into pointless and toxic conversations anymore.

Do you find yourself being talked over or interrupted when you are trying to get your point across? It is frustrating and what you might find yourself doing is raising your voice or starting to interrupt the other person to try to get back into the conversation. The other person however is likely to do the same, and in the end neither is listening, both fighting for space, and the relationship may be fraught with tension. It is a common conversational trap, but there is a way out. The secret is to talk about your talking. In future, instead of just saying the thing you want to say, you first talk about what is going on between you. Instead of launching straight in, talk about what it is you are wanting to do. 'I've got something I want to say, it will take me a couple of minutes, so if you are willing to hear me out, I'll say what it is. Give me time to finish what I want to say and then I'll listen to what you think in response.' It might sound obvious, but how many times in the past would that have been a helpful strategy?

As you practise the skills of talking about your talking, what you will see is that it slows you down, curbs your impulse to jump into the fray, and that instead of fighting for attention, you create space for yourself to move into. Perhaps now the parallel I was making earlier between psychotherapy and martial arts is clearer. You learn to respond, rather than react to situations.

In everyday life, we will be faced every so often with important decisions about new challenges, such as whether to apply for a new job or start a new course. Taking on such challenges is an important part of growing and developing as a person. The more we can test our limits and capabilities, the more we will learn about ourselves. New challenges are opportunities for us. However, we don't always see it that way. When we take on new challenges, we also must face the possibility of failure. Rather than seeing the opportunity in the situation, we often focus on what it will be like to fail. As a result, embarking on a new challenge can be frightening, and the fear of failure can be too much to bear. In these cases, we may avoid the challenge altogether and carry on down the same path we were on. We make excuses to ourselves so that we can stay in our comfort zone. But the truth is that staying in your comfort zone – particularly when you do so out of fear – is not always exactly comfortable. By avoiding challenges, we don't have the opportunities to learn about ourselves. We feel trapped – as if we were leading a life that is not true to ourselves. We are plagued by discomfort, anxiety and the niggling sense that things are not quite right.

There are times and places when we might want to avoid a challenge for good, realistic reasons. The trouble comes, however, when we don't recognise that we are making excuses. Perhaps, deep down, we are frightened of what we might learn about ourselves. But instead of acknowledging that, we tell ourselves that now is not a good time, or that this isn't the right opportunity. In reality, it is our fear talking. Taking on new challenges will stretch us and give us more opportunities to be ourselves. The question is not how to lead a life in which we never feel the fear of failure, but rather, how we can move forward despite our fear. Are we able to transform our fear into an enthusiasm to engage with the new challenge and learn from it?

What I am suggesting is that we deliberately look for unusual and perspective-changing experiences, no matter how small. The key is to be open to learning from our experiences, able to let go of old ways of thinking and feeling as new information comes to light, and always seeking to become fuller and more developed versions of ourselves. Real therapeutic change involves thinking deeply about who you are and making the effort to peel away layers of denial, delusion and defence. It is long past time to embrace the demise of that false picture of the self and welcome the emergence of a new and yet unknown version of who we are. But learning about ourselves is challenging. If we are to move forward, we must be able to forgive ourselves for not knowing yesterday what we know today.

Finally, I want to return to something else that Bruce Lee would tell his students, a Zen parable in which a man consults a Zen master. As the master is talking, he is often interrupted by the man who, it is clear to the Zen master, is only hearing what he already knows. So, the Zen master begins to pour the tea. The cup fills but the Zen master keeps pouring such that the cup overflows. 'It's full!' the man exclaims. 'Like you,' the master replies. 'How can I teach you until you empty your cup?'

We need to approach life in this way, receptive and open to learning. Only that way can we learn to be fully present in the moment, the topic of the next chapter.

5

Becoming Lives

'The good life is a process, not a state of
being. It is a direction, not a destination.'

Jack was one of the first clients I had as a young trainee therapist in my early thirties. He was in his seventies and had recently lost his wife to cancer. I remember looking out of my window and watching him approach my counselling room, slightly stooped because of his arthritis and walking slowly with a stick. I can't remember much of the sessions we had together. I am sure I did my best as a young therapist but looking back now, over a quarter of a century later, I feel that I was simply out of my depth. How could I, at the age I was then, truly appreciate the very heavy weight he was carrying, of having lived a life to the age he was, with all his experiences of ageing and decline and the loss of a lifetime companion? As I look back on my younger self, I feel ashamed of my attempts to be a therapist, and sadness that no matter how much I was eager to help, the fact is that it was completely beyond my understanding. How could I have understood enough about what life is like to have been able to reach out fully with compassion and empathy to this man, so lost in his loneliness and grief?

Our sessions together finished, and for the last time I watched Jack from my window as he walked steadily away, hunched over, into the early evening. I have always remembered him because he gave me one of my first experiences as a therapist, and although I didn't know it at the time, he gave me a gift that over the years I have slowly unwrapped, which is an understanding that therapy is most often about the very ordinariness of life. It is about appreciating the profundity of being alive, the frailty of existence, the ever-present lurking figure of death and being able to be present with another human being in their darkest moments.

Jack has stuck in my memory for all this time, and as each year passes, my feelings of sadness have grown about how ill-equipped I was to meet the weight of the loss that he carried. I was doing all I could at the time, but it is simply a fact that therapists can only go as far as they are able to go. If I was to meet Jack as the person I am today, I would understand his burden in a very different way, with a much deeper ability to empathise with him. Almost thirty years on, I understand so much more about loss than I did then. Loss is not something that can be fixed for a person; understanding, empathy, compassion are all that clients often need from a therapist. As easy as that might sound, I think it takes most of us the best part of a lifetime and a dedication to our own personal growth to be able to make a difference.

Am I saying that a person can't be a psychotherapist until they are beyond a certain age? Not at all. Psychotherapists provide a lot of different services, but when it comes to the big questions of life, it makes a difference if your therapist has faced some of those challenges for themselves. Becoming a psychotherapist is a lifelong pursuit, not one that ends with the award of a qualification. Living gives a person the opportunity to experience things, both good and bad, but of course the fact of ageing is itself no guarantee of wisdom. It is not just about encountering events in one's life that is important, but how one engages with the challenges that they present, and the willingness to see the opportunities for learning about oneself.

What I hadn't fully appreciated those many years ago when I met Jack was that by sitting and listening to other people's stories, their tragedies and struggles with life, I was on the road of my own personal growth. Clients take their therapists to new places and Jack took me to a place that at my young age I didn't know, but through him I began to learn something for myself. So it is that therapists through their experience have the opportunity to go on long journeys of discovery about themselves. This might surprise some people. I've often been asked how I cope with listening to people's stories of trauma and tragedy. It is assumed that it must be hard to do, upsetting, difficult. Certainly, it can be heart-wrenching at times, but it can also be life-affirming, and a powerful way to be reminded of what really matters.

For me, the main lesson has been learning that we are all somewhere along our own journey through life, and that each of us must work out for ourselves where we are and what it means for us. I have also learned that as a therapist I can't make people happy or take away their pain, and the more I try to do this, the more I probably get in that person's way of working it out for themselves.

As the opening quote from the psychologist Carl Rogers at the top of this chapter says, the good life is a direction, not a destination. He also went on to say 'This process of the good life is not, I am convinced, a life for the faint-hearted. It involves the stretching and growing of becoming more and more of one's potentialities. It involves the courage to be. It means launching oneself fully into the stream of life. Yet the deeply exciting thing about human beings is that when the individual is inwardly free, he chooses as the good life this process of becoming.'

This is a description of when people are at their best, living their life to their full potential, doing things that they find meaningful and purposeful, feeling pleasure and joy in their activities, and engaged in rewarding and intimate relationships. Each of us is seeking such a life, asking ourselves what our goals are, trying to find our purpose and struggling with despair when the answers to our questions cannot be found. What we learn is that happiness is not a destination but a direction.

How often have we heard the adage that happiness is a direction, not a destination? I have heard it many times and spent a career studying happiness to know that it is true. Yet, I look back on my life and I can see that for much of it I was living it as if what I was doing today was only valuable for what it would bring tomorrow. The idea that the good life is a process rather than an outcome though is not a new idea. Happiness isn't something that happens to us, it is not something external to us that we find along the way; it is about how we engage with our existence, the stance we take towards life and, as Carl Rogers wrote, the courage to be, to understand life as a process. Until we learn that, happiness will always be elusive. I think we have the wisdom inside ourselves to know this, and with the right questions we can get more in tune with ourselves and our deeper wisdom of how a good life should be lived.

*

Imagine yourself in your eighties, sitting in a rocking chair looking back on your life. What would that older you say to you right now?

People want to be happy, but paradoxically, most of us seem to pursue just the opposite. It has been said that 'it is the very pursuit of happiness that thwarts happiness'.[1] When we seek happiness as a destination, we forgo the opportunity to experience the journey itself. We often pursue a life of happiness as an end goal, doing things today in the belief that it will bring happiness tomorrow, but that is like seeking the end of a rainbow; it can't be found. Deep down, we may know this already, but nonetheless much time is spent chasing these rainbows.

It is a mistake to live life with your thoughts always on the future, chasing happiness, but this does not mean that we ought to live solely in the present pursuing pleasure. Pleasure is an important part of life, but when it becomes the only goal of our lives the benefits quickly fade. If you like chocolate, you know how great the first few chunks are, but too much and you will tire of it and soon feel ill. It's all about balance.

Think of Huxley's seminal novel, *Brave New World*, and its warning of a society in which its citizens get lost in pleasure from overindulgence in sex and taking the drug soma, oblivious to the concerns of the world around them.[2] I'm not saying that we are living in Huxley's world, yet we are not that far from it. Consider the mass consumption of alcohol and other drugs available to help numb us, the mindless waste of our lives that a lot of television or social media is. I am also pretty sure no one has ever said on their deathbed that they wish they had watched more television or spent more time online.

In their quest to understand what makes people happy, today's psychologists have begun to look back at the ancient writings of the Greek philosopher Aristotle.[3] In the fourth century bce, Aristotle proposed the concept of *eudaimonia* (pronounced you-day-monia) in his *Nicomachean Ethics*. The term *eudaimonia* is etymologically based in the Greek words *eu* (good) and *daimon* (spirit). It describes the notion that living in accordance with one's *daimon*, which we take to mean character and virtue, leads to a good life. In essence, just as an acorn has within it the potential to be an oak tree – and only an oak tree, not any other type of tree, or a bird or a daffodil – each human being has the potential to be a person, not anything else. And inherent in each person is a unique set of potentials.

To realise our potential, we need what Aristotle called 'real goods'. By this, he meant those things necessary for the development of our potential, such as shelter, clothing, food and friends, but also arts, music, literature and culture. In the modern world, there are certain things that we need to have to be able to pursue the fulfilment of our individual potential. In this sense, real goods are defined by their necessity to us as individuals.

The obvious example is that we need money, and so it becomes a real good. But there is also what Aristotle referred to as the 'golden mean', which is the right amount of the good: too little and we are in deficit of what we need to pursue our potential, as in times of famine when people's potential is literally thwarted; too much and what was a real good becomes an 'apparent good' – something we don't need. Apparent goods may give us pleasure, but we don't *need* them. The important thing is not to confuse them with real goods, as they are not essential to us.

Modern-day positive psychologists are now taking these ideas based on ancient Greek philosophy very seriously in their quest to understand what seems most important for a good life. What has become such a huge problem for many of us is that our lives are filled with apparent goods. Modern life makes it hard to find happiness because we end up striving and investing our energies in the quest for apparent goods.

Similar ideas were expressed centuries after Aristotle by the pioneering humanistic psychologist Eric Fromm, in his classic book *To Have or To Be?*. Fromm wrote about 'having' and 'being' as two different mindsets or attitudes towards life. He wrote about how having was a dominant cultural mindset and ultimately at the root of so much of our personal and social problems. I was reminded of Fromm's book recently when by chance I heard on the radio a most striking and beautiful piece of music. I didn't know what it was, and I started listening intently, letting it soak into me, but then I noticed that my mind was wandering as if somehow to own the music, to possess it. It was like it wasn't enough for me just to enjoy the moment – I needed to memorise, understand and analyse what I was hearing, to be able to capture that moment. And in doing this, I was no longer enjoying it. I wasn't even really listening anymore. I was no longer just in that moment with the music flowing into me. What stopped me from being in that moment? The answer is that the having mindset is so deeply ingrained within me, as with many of us, that it can take over and push our being out of the way.

The having mindset poses an essential problem for humanity. Fromm writes about how it derives from our materialistic culture in which having as a mindset is prioritised over a being mindset. As I talked about earlier, most of us will learn as children that our lives are measured by our achievements, in exams and sports, positions and awards and, as we grow older, by our careers. We learn to value ourselves only in terms of others' expectations.

Usually, this is in terms of our ability to produce monetary reward. I see this every day in my job as a university professor. My colleagues and I are interested in helping the young people we work with develop and mature not only intellectually but personally. We see the opportunities that university can offer for people to become more rounded, fully functioning people. But university courses are ranked not in terms of the personal development and emotional maturity that they help to facilitate in their students, but in terms of the students' employability and their earnings after graduation. This is important too, but should it be the sole criterion or the most important one? In whose interest is the having mindset?

The having mindset is not good for our well-being. Since the pioneering work of Fromm, many other psychologists have gone on to discuss how a more materialistic attitude to life is damaging to us, in terms of contributing to a range of psychological dysfunctions, such as depression and anxiety. But even if a person doesn't suffer from severe psychological problems, at the very least a materialistic attitude will be an obstacle to developing into a fully formed and mature human being. One of the psychologists whose work I most admire is Tim Kasser. For more than two decades, he and his colleagues have been studying people's values and goals and how they relate to the good life.[4] Kasser refers to it as living the 'goods life'.

They have described two types of goals and values. First, those that arise when people 'buy into' the messages of consumer culture and organise their lives around the pursuit of money, possessions, image and status. These goals are said to be *extrinsic* because they are focused on the attainment of external rewards and praise and are typically means to some other end. Second, those goals and values involving striving for personal growth, intimacy and contribution to the community. These goals are said to be *intrinsic* because they are inherently more satisfying to pursue and are more likely to satisfy deeper psychological needs. People feel motivated by intrinsic goals. Numerous studies have found that the extent to which people prioritise intrinsic over extrinsic goals is associated with higher levels of vitality and life satisfaction, and with lower levels of depression and anxiety.

But more than that, when we are able to follow our intrinsic motivations we move towards greater *self-actualisation*, the term used by the famous psychologist Abraham Maslow to describe the state in which we are fulfilled in our potential to be the best version of ourselves.[5] The self-actualised person has many of those qualities that I have been describing throughout this book. They are appreciative of life. They accept themselves and others. They have a sense of agency in life. They have meaningful relationships but are not reliant on others as external sources of influence. They trust their own perceptions. They perceive reality as realistically as it possible to do and are not biased in their judgements of situations or themselves.

Self-actualisation is to be welcomed, but to return to the
theme of this chapter, it is not helpful to think of it as an end
point that we have either achieved or not; rather it best seen
as a process of becoming that we are always engaged in and
moving towards, a process that we take pleasure in as we
experience ourselves as growing and developing.

It often seems to me that most of us treat life as if we were
just playing a giant game of Monopoly in real time. Which of
us can amass the most wealth and property and exploit the
other players? I remember the delight of playing monopoly
as a child, how exciting it was when I was doing well, but
the misery and tears when it was going badly. Remember
what it was like if you were one of the players that ran out of
money and had to leave the game, or when you were going
round the board hoping for a bit of luck just to stay afloat?
We seem to have taken the experience of being alive with
all its joys and opportunities for personal development and
turned it into a dehumanising game. It is a game in which
we learn to value only what brings us monetary gain. Earlier
I talked about personal power, the psychology of which is
often used in some self-help books to show us how to play
this game better, but how I see it is that those with personal
power can choose not to play this game at all.

The emotional fallout from consumer culture is very real,
but people rarely connect how they are feeling to the ways

in which they look at the world and the values they choose to hold. We truly need so little in the way of material things to be contented with life. We need a sense of purpose, meaning, relationships, a sense of agency, good health and the resources to be safe and secure. No one needs a million-dollar painting on their wall, these things by themselves will not bring greater contentment. A belief that they do is an illusion held by those with the having mindset. Why then are we so easily drawn to this? As I've talked about, this is a way of keeping ourselves busy, distracted and our gaze averted from the more important task of working out how to spend our lives wisely in the face of impending death.[6] I use the term spend our lives deliberately, as it does seem as if time is our true currency.

It is difficult not to succumb to the having mindset to some degree as it is how society's systems are organised. But that is a political choice in which we all have a say at each election whether to vote for those who want to take us further down that path or for those who propose a different currency. And in the meantime, it is a personal choice how much we give our lives away to consumer culture.

The best wisdom from psychotherapy shows us that the good life is to understand it as a process of personal growth. From the Greek philosophers to the modern-day positive psychologists, all agree that it is the human condition to always be striving for personal growth, or to put it another way, to be better versions of ourselves. Understanding life in this way is something people must come to on their own, when they are ready. It can't be taught. We must learn this for ourselves. As a Tibetan proverb says: 'Seeking happiness outside ourselves is like waiting for sunshine in a cave facing north.'

The Danish philosopher Søren Kierkegaard said that the aim of life is 'to be that self which one truly is'. As a psychotherapist I see this longing in people to be themselves, although it may not be explicitly expressed like that. Patients plead for help to deal with their depression or their anxiety, but as I listen to their stories what I hear is a deep longing simply to be themselves and the freedom to choose how to live their life, in a way that allows them to be more fully rounded versions of who they are. You know this is true for yourself, but chances are you don't know what to do about it. Carl Rogers helped us first understand that no matter what the issues seemed to be on the surface, all clients were essentially dealing with the existential issue of how to be themselves. As therapy progresses he observed a general tendency for clients to change in ten directions.[7]

First, people move in a direction that is away from facades. No longer willing to put on a metaphorical mask, people become more willing to be open about who they are, what they think and how they are feeling.

Second, no longer driven by 'oughts', people begin to live

life as they see it rather than how they have been instructed by others about how they ought to be.

Third, no longer willing to do what others expect of them, people move away from living a life driven by others' expectations.

Fourth, no longer willing to spend their days pleasing others, people begin doing what pleases them.

Fifth, people move towards self-direction. They begin to choose their own paths in life and their own goals.

Sixth, people become aware that they are not fixed in who they are, but that life is an ever-changing adventure, where things change in new and exciting ways, and where one is always learning.

Seventh, people's eyes are opened to the complexities of the world and of themselves as part of it. No longer content with the old certainties, people begin to embrace the richness of life.

Eighth, people move towards openness to experience, seeking to learn and to change and to enjoy the challenges ahead.

Ninth, people become more accepting of others. As they become more open to themselves, they become more open to others.

Finally, people become more trusting of themselves, daring to feel their own feelings and to trust their own sense of themselves and their uniqueness in the world.

In this way, Rogers' view was that the good life is not an outcome to be achieved, once and for all, but rather it is a process that we must be constantly engaged with and to be continually moving towards. Most importantly, however, it is about having the freedom to move in any direction. What that freedom looks like will be different to each person. Amanda, who we have met previously, and who had gone from one job to another throughout her career without ever finding a direction that felt true to who she was, was initially devastated when she was dismissed from her job, but over time she began to use the opportunity to learn more about herself and became increasingly interested in developing and changing as a person. She was curious about how she was becoming more in touch with her feelings and how she could use them to guide her, to be able to express herself and her feelings openly and honestly. This led her to see how her experience had opened the door to new opportunities. Finding what really matters to her led Amanda to understand how she had so easily bought into the values of her parents, her religion and a culture of success and materialism. By becoming active in local politics and writing about environmental issues, she found something that meant more to her. She realised that the direction her life had been taking wasn't fitting for her, and she found something that was more valuable and meaningful to her.

Amanda's story is not unusual. Most of us, to some extent,

get caught up in a culture of success and materialism. It is not possessions in themselves that are the problem: the problem is when we over prioritise their importance in our lives. Rather than being the means to an end, they become the end.

It is possible to sleepwalk through our lives without ever realising what really matters to us or learning to live in a way that satisfies any of our deep-seated dreams. Many people have a niggling sense that things could be different, but don't do anything about it. It is a mistake to think of happiness as something that can ever be attained as a permanent state of being, but rather it is wise to understand it as a process that we are engaged in from day to day. This involves the ability to be able to be present in the moments of your life. Rogers described what he called 'organismic valuing', which many psychologists now call mindfulness, and involves our ability to stay tuned into our bodies and our feelings.

I mentioned before the idea that our bodies can be cleverer than our minds in giving us clues about what direction to move in. In day-to-day life, it is easy to switch off such that we are not aware of our bodies, our breathing, whether our muscles are tense, the feel of the sun or the wind on our skin, whatever smells and aromas are around us, but in becoming more able to be present, this all changes; we become aware of ourselves as physical creatures. If we only live in our heads, we are disconnected from the deeper wisdom we have within us. We need to learn to be accepting of our bodies and connected to all parts of ourselves.

When we become attentive to our thoughts and feelings in this different way, we are more determined to understand ourselves. We will use more precise language to talk about how we are feeling. We will notice when our attention wanders and develop our ability to stay focused. And very importantly, we will begin to develop and deepen our ability to observe ourselves, others and situations without judgement.

In this way, our map of the world and of ourselves becomes less rigid, open to new interpretations, understandings and constructions of how to perceive the world and ourselves. Our thoughts and feelings about ourselves, our beliefs and opinions about the world and our place in it, all of these make up who we are, and we must be ready to abandon all of them in favour of more realistic perceptions. The process I am describing involves the change in who you are. As I have already discussed, this can come about following sudden and shocking events in our lives that shatter our preconceptions, razing them to the ground, leaving us no choice but to rebuild a new version of ourselves; or it can be a longer process in which, as in therapy, we gradually dismantle our preconceptions and slowly remodel and rebuild.

But even as I write this, I realise that the way people often talk about therapy makes it sound like we can change our lives without changing ourselves. Sometimes it seems like we think of ourselves as a little person at the steering wheel of a car. When we think about personal change, we think it is like getting a new car. We can trade in the old one with all its dents and scratches and drive out of the forecourt anew. But we imagine that we are still inside driving it just as we were. What I'm saying is that there is no little person inside, we are more like a self-driving car. We can't remain exactly the person we are right now and also change.

That's what makes personal growth so frightening to people. To change, we need to assume that we can be a better and more beautiful version of ourselves, that this will be worthwhile to pursue and that it is a lifelong journey. The implication is that we are not all we could be, that we will need to acknowledge our weaknesses as well as our strengths, our failures as well as our successes.

Developing ourselves in this way, we can become someone who can treat events in our lives as learning opportunities. We won't feel that we are in competition with others and always trying to prove ourselves. When we meet new people, we will be interested in them and what they have to say. We won't feel the need to score points or try to be cleverer than them, but instead we will be open to learning from them. Our gaze and attention are turned towards the other person, not inwards to ourselves and our own internal thoughts. In that way, we can truly see the other person. Unfortunately, such people are rare and when we meet them, unless we too are similarly attentive, we can miss them. They may be the quiet ones, listening to and observing the world around them, while the more outspoken and attention-grabbing people take the limelight.

They are not simply people who are adjusted to their culture, but able to live within it, often harmoniously. But they do not conform. They will seek to balance their own needs for autonomy in a socially constructive way that takes into consideration the needs of others. Such people will be more determined to do their own thing, whatever it is that is right for them, but not in a way that tramples over others. And they will not bend easily to others who want to trample over them.

Such people are also more creative, in the sense of how they approach life. In some ways, it is fair to say that creativity is what arises out of psychotherapy, but the therapist is not trying to make this happen. It is just what happens when someone feels truly listened to and understood, they drop their defences, become more able to think about whatever is troubling them and look at things from new perspectives.

But the effects of such a change in how one approaches life will be profound, in how we feel about our activities, as we will feel more alive, involved, that we are being true to who we are, doing what we were meant to do, complete and fulfilled. Ultimately, it leads to a psychologically richer life. Carl Rogers[8] described how increased openness, adaptability and existential living will be experienced as deeply enriching qualities.

It is only in recent years that psychologists have been referring to the 'psychologically rich life', but it is an idea that has been around for a long time in the personal growth theory of Rogers about what often happens upon encountering new and challenging experiences.

Being open to new experiences fuels personal growth, allowing a person to be more self-determining, thus more able to find meaning and happiness, but also have a more psychologically rich life. Those who have more rigid and fixed ways of thinking and feeling are not as open to new experiences, haven't got the same drive to always be learning about themselves and the world, and consequently will lead less rich lives.

A person can set out to lead a psychologically rich life, but unless they have a high level of personal growth, it is almost impossible. Some people may travel around the world but wherever they go they only ever see the world through their own expectations and preconceptions. A richer life may be had by someone who has travelled less, but wherever they go they try to look through the eyes of those who live there. It is important to be interested in the world around us, follow our curiosity and take time to step outside our own point of view, to take a look from others' viewpoints, to be open to walk in others' shoes. A psychologically rich life arises from new encounters and experiences that challenge us to see things differently and can lead to a profound shift in perspective.

These ideas are supported by recent research. Across four studies,[9] Shigehiro Oishi, a professor of psychology at the University of Virginia, and his colleagues, found that people who reported leading a more psychologically rich life were especially more open to experience. They assessed psychological richness by asking participants questions such as whether they thought their life would make a good movie or asking them if on their deathbed they would be likely to say that their life had been interesting. These are good questions to ask ourselves periodically, as a way of sensing within ourselves if we are on the right track.

Another aspect of becoming more fully functioning is that we become more harmonious with nature, as we come to understand more deeply our connection to and part in the natural world. Rather than seeing the natural world as something separate to ourselves, only useful to own or to use, we can become able to be in nature, in the way that Fromm talked about in his classic book *To Have or to Be?*. The person who is fully functioning is invested in environmental, social and political happenings in the world. We are in touch with the rhythm of nature when we are in touch with our true selves.

Research supports this idea. In one intriguing study it

was found that those who scored higher on a test for being more authentic and genuine also showed more connectedness to nature, love and care for nature, and were more likely to use products that are environmentally friendly.[10] This suggests that destructive environmental behaviours may be the result of how far people have become alienated from themselves. Such a view echoes ideas that will be familiar to those versed in Buddhist wisdom and philosophies. Beth Kempton[11] writes: 'The forest does not care what your hair looks like. The mountains don't move for any job title. The rivers keep running, regardless of your social media following, your salary or your popularity. The flowers keep on blooming, whether or not you make mistakes. Nature just is, and welcomes you, just as you are.'

We need to be able to live in the present moment, to be aware of what's going on around us, and enjoy our lives as they unfold in the moment. But instead our thoughts are often away in some imagined future, either one that we are looking forward to or one that we wish to avoid. For many of us, imagined fears about what might happen are all too common and keep us awake in the small hours of the night. For others, it is sadness or anger about something that has happened in their past. And in that way, we fail to be present in our lives and appreciate the people around us, and the joy and purpose of what's going on in the moment.

I've learned that I can choose to be more present in the here and now. One piece of advice I have always found useful is something written by the self-help author Dale Carnegie who proposed that we think of our days as like the separate sections of an ocean liner, each separated from the next by a watertight bulkhead. He talked about it as living in 'day-tight compartments'.[12] Keep today sealed, such that the sadness and anger about yesterday and the fears about tomorrow can't leak in.

Becoming fully ourselves is a lifelong project, in which we find joy in learning about ourselves, but one of the biggest learnings is that what really matters is not what we can get for ourselves but what we can give to others. When people can find their own direction in life – when they become more intrinsically motivated – there are benefits not only for themselves but also to those around them. People who organise their lives around intrinsic values have been shown to treat others in more humane ways and pursue more collectively minded lifestyles. Living in accordance with intrinsic values is therefore good not only for those people themselves but also for the rest of us.

6

Not Just You

'Other people matter.'

This quote has stuck in my mind since I first heard the late positive psychologist Chris Peterson say it. In three words, it captures very powerfully what seems like an appropriate and most important final lesson, one that is vital to us as human beings if we want to live a good life, that other people matter. I've placed it as the final lesson in this book because I think it arises out of the other lessons. I don't think we can just decide that other people are important until we feel that we ourselves are. When we truly value ourselves, we value other people as well. We understand that life can be hard and that each of us is doing our best, which allows us to replace our judgements with compassion.

I also wanted to include Peterson's quote because I was

fond of him, not that I knew him well. I only met him a few times at conferences, yet my meetings with him stayed with me, because he was a gentle and kind person. I knew him well, however, through his work. A professor of psychology at the University of Michigan, he was well known for his work on optimism.[1] As a student in the 1980s, I had been inspired by Peterson's work when doing my own doctorate research, and later as a lecturer, in the years before I met him, I had used his textbook about clinical psychology in my classes. I greatly admired him. I looked up to and was inspired by him. I saw him as a role model. So when he died at the very young age of 62 in 2012,[2] it came as a powerful reminder to me about how life is not to be taken for granted. As I approach that age myself, I very often think of Peterson when I find myself making plans; he's like a wise and friendly figure, sitting nearby, reminding me to not lose sight of what really matters. That other people matter.

So much of what I've said so far in this book has been about the lessons we can learn for ourselves, that it might sound like I am encouraging people only to think selfishly. The opposite is true. As we mature emotionally and grow as people, we also develop our sense of responsibility to others and are more inclined towards more giving and considerate attitudes. Not only that, as we gain in our own personal power, we become more successful in life, whatever that might look like for each of us, and in our own ways have more to give. One of the trade-offs is often that we acquire greater social power. We find ourselves in positions of greater influence that require us to manage, supervise and lead others. But social power can corrupt some people. The challenge of social power is to use it to nurture and grow the personal power not only of yourself but of others. Rather than *power-over* others, we ought to use our *power-for* others, to use it to help those in need and to build them up. Making other people matter in our lives is one of the most important things we can do, and I think it is part and parcel of what happens when we begin to re-examine our own priorities.

I had a personal revelation about a decade ago when I was taking part in a workshop on personal growth. It ran over several days and involved the small group of participants getting to know each other through sharing life experiences and engaging in challenging conversations. On the final day, the facilitator asked those present to, in turn, say to the person on the right of them what positive qualities they had brought to the sessions. Everyone obliged. When the person on my left turned to me, she told me how much she appreciated my intellect, my curiosity and my love of learning. I was pleased – as you might expect in someone who grew up with a need to do well in school. This was like a gold star for me. But then I heard someone else in the group who I admired being told that they were valued for their warmth, kindness and compassion. It was in that moment I realised that what I thought I valued in myself was not what I really valued, at least not anymore; what I really valued were these other qualities of warmth, kindness and compassion. Until that point, I hadn't realised that this was more important to me and from that moment, I was determined to cultivate these qualities in myself and make these my priority in life.

Imagine someone you respect was to turn to you, right now, and tell you what it is about you that they admire. What do you think they might say? What would you like them to say?

We also know the importance of our connections to others from the many research studies into how people change following trauma and tragedy, which I mentioned earlier. It is one of the defining features of posttraumatic growth that people come to appreciate and value their relationships so much more and desire more genuine and deeper connections with others. It is our connections to others, our memories of being with others, that we appreciate the most when we are faced with adversity. What really matters in life is ultimately other people. Remember in *A Christmas Carol* how Scrooge, reminded of his mortality, is transformed on awakening on Christmas morning? The difference is in how he behaves with those around him. He becomes more appreciative and kind. He decides to give his employee a huge rise in salary.

He buys a turkey for his employee's family. Evidence suggests that this is not just a nice story. People genuinely become more giving when confronted with mortality. In one study, for example, it was found that when people were interviewed close to a funeral home, they were more likely to give to charity when later asked. The authors called this the 'Scrooge effect'.[3] When we live a life that matters, our relationships are one of the first things to blossom.

A more modern take on the story of Scrooge is in the 1993 movie *Groundhog Day*. Brent Dean Robbins, a humanistic psychologist, has an interesting take on how it is a lesson in happiness.[4] It centres around character Phil Connors, played by Bill Murray, who is caught in what seems like an endless loop in time in which he wakes up each morning to relive the same day. It seems like a form of purgatory, but it gives Phil the opportunity to experiment with what brings him happiness. Robbins describes how at first Phil does all the typical things people might do to make themselves happy, such as stuffing his face with food, which at first seems like fun, but over time becomes tedious. He learns that simply seeking to maximise one's own pleasure doesn't work. As time goes on, he comes instead to experiment with trying out more altruistic and creative ways of living. He takes up the piano, helps other people, and in so doing fosters a sense of belonging and community. Only then is he able to feel a more genuine sense of fulfilment. It is as though he has been put in this endless loop to learn this lesson about what really matters for a good life.

By nature, we are social animals, and it is in our relationships with others that we can express ourselves and have our needs met. But if we only understand our relationships in terms of what we get out of them, we are missing the point. Relationships are reciprocal and the way in which they matter includes what we give to them. But what *really* matters is much more than simply thinking about giving and getting. If we only understand our relationships in terms of giving and getting, we get stuck in a mindset where all we see is cost-benefit transactions rather than the true value of living in relationships with other people. Unfortunately, I think it is too easy for us to get trapped in this mindset where we treat our relationships with others in this commodified way, losing sight of our own humanity and that of others.

In contrast, in Buddhism, as well as in psychotherapy, the key to genuine relationships is approaching life with a non-judgemental way of being: to be with others in such a way that you place no expectations or demands on them to be different to who they are. For me, when we talk about other people mattering, that is what it means. For that to happen we need to be able to develop an attitude of unconditional acceptance towards others. Before I talked about unconditional self-regard, but now I'm talking about unconditional regard *for others*, where it is OK for us to be in relationships with no other agenda to manipulate, control or coerce other people for our gain or benefit. We can simply be with others and value them just as they are. That is of course how we want other people to treat us.

Earlier I talked about how conditional regard from others can be so damaging to us; here I want to consider when we are those others – the parents, teachers, lecturers, church leaders or whoever – and the importance of us being that person who takes an unconditional attitude towards others. When our regard for others is conditional, we see them only in relation to what we want from them and what they can do for us, or for how well they live up to our expectations. Such relationships lack sincerity and can never be truly enriching. Think about your relationships with those closest to you. If you have children, you are likely to have hopes and dreams for them, but do you communicate with them in such a way that they understand that you value and love them regardless of how well they live up to your hopes and dreams for them? Or is it possible that they feel you love and value them only insofar as they are achieving the hopes and dreams you have for them? That is a tough question that demands some real honesty. Similarly, with our partners or close friends, how much are we able to develop truly unconditional attitudes towards them, in which they feel accepted by us regardless of their mood, appearance, success or whatever? When we analyse the nature of many of our relationships, we may realise quite how conditional we are in our love and valuing of those others. It can be subtle but nonetheless it happens. If we truly believe that other people matter, it must be for who they are, not for who we want them to be.

We are all just another person to everyone else, so in saying 'other people matter', we are also saying that we want to matter to others. We can learn to value other people, but we can't make other people value us. Many of the values we are conditional about are not of our own making but reflect society. We live in a culture of conditionality, with different groups, defined by political views and religious beliefs, for example, competing for power over how to define the conditions by which others will be valued. It is easy to take our own culture for granted just as it is, and not to question the ideas and beliefs that shape us. Look for example at how in recent years we have become a more accepting society in terms of gender and sexuality, and with hindsight it is easy to see what it must have been like in the past to live in a society that marginalised all who did not identify with traditional gender roles, or what were seen as acceptable sexual preferences. In every way imaginable, people were being told how they needed to be, to be valued. Only with the perspective of history can we see clearly just how conditional society was. The challenge is to understand the ways in which society remains conditional in the present day in its valuing of people. Conditional regard is judgemental. It damages people psychologically. When we think about ourselves, we want to be accepted unconditionally.

If we wish to be accepted unconditionally by others, surely, we must live by example. But acceptance and compassion for others starts with acceptance and compassion for ourselves. Psychologists have known for a long time that those who are more accepting of themselves are more accepting of others, and that those who have a low opinion of themselves tend to reject others.[5] Early in the twentieth century, the Austrian psychotherapist Alfred Adler proposed that a tendency to disparage others arose out of feelings of inferiority as an overcompensation.[6] In the aftermath of the Second World War, Eric Fromm wrote about how the hostility towards Jews in Germany was related to a cultural self-rejection,[7] and we must ask whether something similar is taking place in the modern world as we see various groups of people facing rejection and disparagement by others.

Mahatma Gandhi is often quoted as having said, 'You must be the change you wish to see in the world'. Whether he actually ever used these precise words, Gandhi's teaching was that whatever changes we would like to see in society have to begin with us. He is reported to have said: 'We but mirror the world. All the tendencies present in the outer world are to be found in the world of our body. If we could change ourselves, the tendencies in the world would also change. As a man changes his own nature, so does the attitude of the world change towards him. This is the divine mystery supreme. A wonderful thing it is and the source of our happiness. We need not wait to see what others do.'

One story goes that a mother was seeking advice from Gandhi to help her son stop eating sugar, but instead of giving her advice on the spot, Gandhi asked her to return in two weeks and said he would speak to the boy then. In two weeks, the mother and son returned, at which time Gandhi spoke with the boy. Afterwards, the mother asked him why he hadn't been able to offer his advice the first time. Gandhi replied, 'Upon your visit two weeks ago I too was eating sugar.' I don't know how true that story is, but it works to illustrate the point that we must be the change we want to see.

I can't imagine anyone who deep down doesn't crave to be unconditionally accepted, in such a way that they are free to live their life in the way they choose, to find their own directions in life without being coerced or controlled by others. If that is the change we want to see, surely it must start with us. We must be the ones that make it a more accepting and compassionate world. We do not need to give back to the world what we ourselves have been given – one might imagine that Nelson Mandela, who spent many of his twenty-seven years in prison breaking rocks into gravel, would have more cause than most to turn his mind to revenge and hatred, but instead he became a peacemaker and unifier. He became president of South Africa, and an example to all of us of the best in human nature.

The very word compassion comes from the Latin word *compati*, 'together with' (*com*), and 'suffer with' (*pati*). How much would you agree with the following statements?[8]

- When I see another person going through a difficult time, I will offer to help.
- I am interested when people talk about their problems.
- When someone makes a mistake, I think to myself that no one's perfect and they still deserve my care.

As already mentioned, when we have compassion for ourselves, we are more likely to have it for others.[9] The benefits of self-compassion are well documented, and include much better psychological health, but it is interesting to see how self-compassion leads to compassion for others. Kristin Neff, at the University of Texas at Austin, and her colleagues,[10] carried out an ingenious experiment in which they asked people to imagine taking part in a job interview and to answer typical questions, one of which was what they considered their greatest weakness and to tell of a time when it affected them. The researchers categorised their responses into ones that used more individualistic language (using pronouns such as 'I' and 'me') or more social language (using pronouns such as 'we' and 'our', and words like 'friend' and 'share'). They found that those who were more self-compassionate used less individualistic language and more social language. Their research suggests that those with more self-compassion have a more interconnected view of themselves.

One might therefore expect differences in political views between more compassionate and less compassionate people. There do seem to be differences on the political spectrum between people who hold more individualistic, less compassionate views of humanity and those who hold more collective, compassionate views of humanity. Indeed, Stephen Morris, from the Department of Philosophy at the College of Staten Island, argues that the research shows that a person's ability to experience empathy is associated with their general political attitudes, specifically, that more empathic people have more liberal political views.[11]

Another characteristic that seems to follow when we are accepting of ourselves is a more grateful attitude towards life. Gratitude involves noticing and appreciating the good things that happen to us, both in general, and in response to what others might do for us. Gratitude is one of the most well researched topics in positive psychology, and we know from many research studies that those who are more grateful have greater well-being, are more able to cope with life, sleep better, and have better health. So just for selfish reasons alone it seems worth cultivating a grateful attitude, such that we find ourselves routinely asking: 'What good is there in this situation that I presently cannot see but I can learn from?' To be able to ask ourselves this question when in difficult and challenging situations allows us to find ways forward, but also transforms our emotions in many situations from ones of anxiety and fear to excitement and hope.

An exercise developed by two psychologists, Robert Emmons and Michael McCullough,[12] at the University of California and Miami, respectively, involves writing down each day things for which one is grateful. Make a list of what you feel grateful for today. What are the good things that have happened today that on reflection you are grateful for? This could include people, possessions, memories. Studies show that keeping a gratitude journal like this is beneficial for mental well-being.

Another exercise is to choose just one moment that stands out in your mind which you feel grateful for. It could be from any time in your life. When I do this exercise it takes me to the encouraging words of one of my professors when I was a student at university. I was twenty-one years old and up to that point I had never received much affirmation from anyone in my life, so his words gave me a new confidence and hope for the future. I have always remembered this; it was a fleeting encounter, yet so valuable to me. While I'm sure I fail as much as I succeed, I always remember how important his words were to me and now I do my best to be for others what he was for me.

Many years later I got the opportunity to let this professor know how important his encouragement was to me as a young man. I believe my telling him that meant something to him. Feeling gratitude is important, but so is letting people know of your gratitude. The main thing, however you do it, is to find ways to show your gratitude to the people you love and those who have helped you or meant something to you.

In these ways, the world becomes gentler, and yet I am not naive: there are those who will see a gentler world as a weak one. So, we may be the change we want to see but it will be no overnight revolution. We also need to engage actively in the world, but to take a gentler approach when we can to our activism.

Sarah Corbett is the author of *How to be Craftivist: The Art of Gentle Protest*[13] and the founder of the global Craftivist Collective. Sarah told me that she used to be an activist working for different charities, but she came to a point where she was feeling burnt out and beginning to doubt the effectiveness of the typical activism tactics that charities and campaign groups used. That led her to adopt a new approach. She now creates craftivism campaigns, to help people learn quiet, kind and creative ways to become change makers. Craftivism is a mix of craft and activism. Sarah says it's like punk music, in that there are lots of different ways people do craftivism. She calls her approach 'gentle protest' where she uses the process of handicrafts to help think slowly, critically and empathetically and uses the products as catalysts for conversation, connection and hopefully positive change.

One piece of Sarah's work that stands out for me is her image of a battered and bruised Barbie doll with tape over her eyes and mouth, holding a small placard that reads: 'You can tell the condition of a nation by looking at the state of its women.' This is a quote from Jawaharlal Nehru, the first prime minister of independent India.[14] Sarah takes such pieces and places them in locations relevant to the issue. Such images can get shared widely attracting interest and sparking new conversations that lead people to think differently.

Most of us only have the resources to do a little to make the world a better place. That might make it seem like it's not worth doing anything, but if we all just did the little bit we could, it would be enough to bring about big changes. Ask yourself every evening, what have I done today to make someone else's life a bit better and brighter? Even the little things count. Sarah encourages us to find ways to build bridges, find common values and connections, to slow down and act thoughtfully, not react aggressively, treat people how we wish to be treated ourselves, and to aspire to a more collective and loving society. I can understand how some might see such an approach as naive, but this gentler approach is where the evidence points. I love the idea of Sarah's 'gentle protest' because I know that changing people's views through shouting, criticising and arguing with them rarely works. As discussed earlier, the more we perceive new information to be a threat to the stories we tell ourselves about who we are, the more we react defensively. People can only take in new information that is inconsistent with their view of themselves when they are in a state of open-mindedness. In the classroom I've learned that giving feedback to students is usually only helpful when they ask for it, and until they ask, they probably won't be ready to receive it. For that to happen they first need to feel accepted.

People become more accepting and empathic towards others if that is how they themselves experience the world, and that must start with each of us. Sarah also reminds us of more words from Mahatma Gandhi: 'When I despair, I remember that all through history, the way of truth and love has always won. There have been tyrants and murderers, and for a time they seem invincible, but in the end, they always fall.'

It is only when we cultivate qualities of kindness, compassion, and forgiveness within ourselves that we can have them for others. In this way, it is through our own personal growth that we can make a better world. We can't be truly happy on our own, and our personal happiness depends as much on the world around us as what we ourselves do. We know from decades of research that people who live in nations characterised by, for example, tolerance, civil rights, absence of corruption, freedom of expression politically and personally, good citizenship, schooling and education are happier.[15] More emotionally mature people know this, they want to create such societies. A good life for everyone means a good life for oneself. It is about recognising that we ourselves are the other people for all those around us. If we want a kinder, compassionate and accepting world, we need to start with ourselves. Each of us is like a stone that creates ripples outwards in a pond.

More than ever there is a need for change that challenges the current values of our society, its materialism, greed, corruption, and the need to think collectively. In a 2011 memorial address for those killed in a mass shooting in Tucson, Arizona, US president Barack Obama said: 'We recognize our own mortality, and we are reminded that in the fleeting time we have on this Earth, what matters is not wealth, or status, or power, or fame – but rather, how well we have loved, and what small part we have played in making the lives of other people better.'[16]

As I come to the end of this chapter, and the end of this book, I want to emphasise that in saying other people matter, I don't mean we need to spend more time socialising or become more extraverted. Relationships with others are important, but we are all different in terms of our need to be with others. For many of us, we may in fact benefit from giving ourselves permission to spend more time in solitude or to embrace time spent alone. Not only that, some of the relationships in our lives may be detrimental to us and we would be better to free ourselves from them.

Personal growth might sound like a selfish thing to pursue, but paradoxically the more developed and emotionally mature we are as people, the more our gaze turns outwards to others, and not because we're trying to find ways to use others to further our own ends, but rather that this is what psychologically well-developed and fully functioning people do. They are caring, compassionate and collectively minded in their views of the world; it is in their nature to be empathic and helpful towards others. And they understand that those who are not like them need empathy and acceptance, not conflict and hostility, if they are, too, to change.

Epilogue

As I come to the end, let me sum up the six lessons of this book.

1. We are all fragile creatures, remember that life is fleeting and precious.
2. Give yourself the greatest gift, learn to value yourself just as you are, no strings attached.
3. Beware of letting yourself be used by others, look to yourself to make the choices in your life that are best for you.
4. Be curious, open to experience, flexible in your thinking, aware of your feelings, and always willing to change your mind, because life is about learning.
5. Enjoy life as it is, be hopeful and work for a better tomorrow, but be content within yourself today.
6. Bring love, kindness, gratitude, understanding and

compassion to the world. In the end that's what
really matters.

These lessons may seem obvious. If you have read some of
the books on happiness that are available, or even just seen
the sheer volume of them out there, you would be forgiven
for thinking that it was all a lot more complicated than this,
but it isn't. Living by these lessons will bring deep personal
change and what Greek philosophers called *phronesis* – a
term which means 'practical wisdom', or that which enables
us to discern and make good judgements about what is the
right thing to do in any given moment, while also knowing
what is worth doing. At first glance, the practical nature of
these lessons may not seem obvious, but you will find that
once they sink deeply into your being, they will provide you
with the wisdom to deal with whatever you encounter.

However, that's not to say that it is easy to do. In the introduction to this book, I talked about these six lessons being
like a balancing pole. I think that is a good metaphor. Many
books will instruct you in what to do to find happiness and
contentment in life. The lessons in this book are not so much
about what to do, as about what stance to take towards life.
If we first develop the right attitude, we begin to see our way
forward more clearly and the right behaviours will follow.
We will be drawn towards what we need to do. We will *know*
what we need to do.

Although I would add that just as it takes time to learn to walk a tightrope, in the same way, it may take time for the lessons I have outlined here to sink in. So, be patient with yourself. These are lessons that philosophers and religious sages have pointed to throughout the ages as vital to a good life, yet they are still so hard to learn and live by. That is not surprising: these are lessons that fly in the face of much of what we will have learned throughout our lives.

Psychologists joke that they study the things that they themselves have difficulties with, and there certainly seems to be some truth to this. Some might say this also applies to me in writing about the good life, just because I am writing about it here, it doesn't mean I've got it all figured out. Like everyone else, I'm trying to work it out. I am a worrier, by nature. I overthink things and I find it hard to live life in the moment. But what I do understand well is that it is not always easy to change the way we are. Pushing ourselves to go faster than we can is usually not helpful. We need to be patient, gentle and kind with ourselves, to accept ourselves unconditionally, knowing that even when we fall, we are doing our best. That's where these lessons come in. So, keep the six truths close to hand for when you need support to help you back on your feet.

Many people want to change their lives, but they don't want to have to change themselves, but unless we change ourselves, the chances are we will find ourselves again and again in similar situations with the same old feelings coming to the surface. The truth is that if we want our lives to change, we need to think about changing ourselves. True happiness is only possible when that is understood. It is up to each of us to make the difference for ourselves. A book can point us in the right direction, but the steps are ours to take for ourselves. Life is precious and fleeting. We can choose to make the most of it, but as the old Chinese proverb says, 'The best time to plant a tree was twenty years ago. The second-best time is now.'

Be compassionate with yourself, allow the lessons to sink gently in, and as you do, I feel sure that you will find the practical wisdom that you are seeking. I hope you have found reading this book as interesting, helpful and enjoyable, as I have writing it.

Let me leave you with three questions.

If you look back on your life so far, which of these six lessons has been the hardest one for you to learn? Think about your answer and why this might be.

Which of these six lessons would be the most useful one for you to learn in your life at the moment? Think about what steps you might take, and what you could do differently, to move forward in your learning.

Are these the six lessons needed for a good life, or would you make some changes to the list? If so, what would your six lessons be?

Acknowledgements

I want to thank the many people who have influenced the stories I've told, and who remain anonymous, and the hundreds of people who have taken part in the research studies mentioned throughout the book. My thanks also to Peter Tallack at the Science Factory for his vision, encouragement and for helping me bring the idea for this book to life; Holly Harley, my editor at Little, Brown, for her enthusiasm, advice and guidance; Elizabeth Dana and James Kingsland, for their helpful notes; Aruna Vasudevan for her skilful copy-editing; Bob Harrison and Sarah Corbett, for their inspiring conversations with me, and my colleagues and friends, especially Rob Hooper, David Murphy, Steve Regel and Joe Sempik. Finally, my thanks to Vanessa Markey for her support and acceptance.

Notes

Author's note

1   The type of psychotherapy I am interested in, and which informs my thinking in this book, follows in the tradition of the American psychologist and psychotherapist Carl Rogers' (1902–1987) client-centred approach to therapy. See: Rogers, C. R. (1951). *Client-Centred Therapy: Its Current Practice, Implications and Theory*. Boston: Houghton Mifflin. For a detailed history and description of this approach, see the biography by Howard Kirschenbaum (2007). *The Life and Work of Carl Rogers*. Ross-on-Wye: PCCS Books. Anyone interested in knowing about the wider field of therapy might find my previous book useful: Joseph, S. (2010). *Theories of Counselling and Psychotherapy: An Introduction to the Different Approaches*. Basingstoke: Palgrave-Macmillan.

Prologue

1 For a discussion about well-being and evidence for its
   parts, see Longo, Y., Coyne, I. & Joseph, S. (2017). 'The
   Scales of General Well-being'. *Personality and Individual
   Differences, 109*, 148-159. This presents the results of an
   investigation into the structure of well-being. We identi-
   fied the fourteen distinct and recurring elements defining
   well-being across the positive psychology literature –
   happiness, vitality, calmness, optimism, involvement,
   self-awareness, self-acceptance, self-worth, competence,
   development, purpose, significance, congruence, and
   connection. For a comprehensive overview of the field,
   see also Maddux, J. E. (2018). *Subjective Well-being and
   Life Satisfaction*. Routledge/Taylor & Francis Group. New
   York and London.

2 The term 'fully functioning' is taken from Carl Rogers
   who used it to describe the characteristics of someone who emerges from therapy. It is someone who is
   always changing, developing and discovering themselves.
   See: Rogers, C. R. (1963). 'The Concept of the Fully
   Functioning Person'. *Psychotherapy: Theory, Research
   & Practice, 1*(1), 17–26. Rogers saw well-being more as
   a process than an outcome and it is this idea that more
   informs this book.

3 Kempton, B. (2018). *Wabi Sabi: Japanese Wisdom for a
   Perfectly Imperfect Life*. London: Piatkus, 175.

4 This description of the process of change is based on the
   work of Carl Rogers, who first recognised this process of

personal growth in the 1950s and developed it into what he called 'client-centred therapy'. This is the type of psychotherapy I specialise in. In this book, I am introducing readers to its most illuminating lessons, but for those who are interested in digging deeper into his work, see Rogers, C. R. (1961). *On Becoming a Person: A Therapist's View of Psychotherapy*. London: Constable. Also, Rogers, C. R. (1959). 'A Theory of Therapy, Personality and Interpersonal Relationships, as Developed in the Client-Centered Framework'. In S. Koch (ed.), *Psychology: A Study of a Science, Vol. 3: Formulations of the Person and the Social Context* (184–256). New York: McGraw Hill.

5   Backing up these ideas is a lot of research showing that the client is the engine of therapy. See Hubble, M. A. & Miller, S. D. (2004). 'The Client: Psychotherapy's Missing Link for Promoting a Positive Psychology'. In P. A. Linley and S. Joseph (eds.), *Positive Psychology in Practice* (335–53). Hoboken: Wiley.

1. Second Life

1   2 Lives. Steven Joel Sotloff Memorial foundation. See https://www.2livesfoundation.org

2   Results showed a significant percentage of survivors were suffering from anxiety and depression symptoms, as well as those of posttraumatic stress. Yule, W., Hodgkinson, P., Joseph, S., Parkes, C. M., & Williams, R. (1990). 'The Herald of Free Enterprise Disaster: 30 Month Follow up'. Paper presented at European conference on traumatic stress, Netherlands, 23–27. See also, Dalgleish, T., Joseph,

S. & Yule, W. (2000). 'The Herald of Free Enterprise Disaster: Lessons from the First 6 Years'. *Behavior Modification, 24*(5), 673–99.

3   Joseph, S., Williams, R. & Yule, W. (1993). 'Changes in Outlook Following Disaster: The Preliminary Development of a Measure To Assess Positive And Negative Responses'. *Journal of Traumatic Stress, 6*(2), 271–9. This was one of the very first scholarly papers to be published on the topic of positive changes following adversity.

4   Joseph, S. (2011). *What Doesn't Kill Us: The New Psychology of Posttraumatic Growth.* New York: Basic Books.

5   The term 'posttraumatic growth' was coined a few years later by two American psychologists Richard Tedeschi and Lawrence Calhoun who had also observed how survivors of trauma often reported positive changes. See Tedeschi, R. G., & Calhoun, L. G. (1995). *Trauma and Transformation.* London: Sage. Also, Tedeschi, R. G., Shakespeare-Finch, J., Taku, K., & Calhoun, L. G. (2018). *Posttraumatic Growth: Theory, Research, and Applications.* New York & London: Routledge/Taylor & Francis.

6   Martin, J., Tolosa, I., & Joseph, S. (2004). 'Adversarial Growth Following Cancer and Support from Health Professionals'. *Health Psychology Update, 13*, 11–17.

7   For a more detailed and deeper dive into the story of Buddha and the influence of Buddhism today, see James Kingsland's 2016 book, *Siddhartha's Brain: The*

Science of Meditation, Mindfulness and Enlightenment.
London: Robinson.

8   Delbo, C. (1995). *Auschwitz and After*. New Haven: Yale
University Press, xvi.

9   See for example, Fung, H. H. & Carstensen, L. L.
(2004). 'Motivational Changes in Response to Blocked
Goals and Foreshortened Time: Testing Alternatives
to Socioemotional Selectivity Theory'. *Psychology and
Aging*, *19*(1), 68–78. Carstensen, L. L., Isaacowitz, D. M.
& Charles, S. T. (1999). 'Taking Time Seriously: A Theory
of Socioemotional Selectivity'. *American Psychologist*,
54(3), 165–81.

10 Solomon, S., Greenberg, J. & Pyszczynski, T. (2015).
The Worm at the Core: On the Role of Death in Life.
London: Penguin.

11 Becker, E. (1973). *The Denial of Death*. New York: Simon
& Schuster.

12 Yalom, I. D. (2011). *Staring at the Sun: Being at Peace with
Your Own Mortality*. London: Piatkus.

13 Wood, A. M., Maltby, J., Stewart, N. & Joseph, S. (2008).
'Conceptualizing Gratitude and Appreciation as a
Unitary Personality Trait'. *Personality and Individual
Differences*, *44*(3), 621–32.

14 Dannenbaum, S. M. & Kinnier, R. T. (2009). 'Imaginal
Relationships with the Dead: Applications for
Psychotherapy'. *Journal of Humanistic Psychology*,
49(1), 100–13.

15 The empty chair technique is mostly associated with the
psychotherapist Fritz Perls and a brand of therapy he

developed, Gestalt therapy. See, Clarkson, P. & Cavicchia, S. (2013). *Gestalt Counselling in Action*. London: Sage.

16   Blackie, L. E., Cozzolino, P. J. & Sedikides, C. (2016). 'Specific and Individuated Death Reflection Fosters Identity Integration'. *PloS one*, *11*(5), e0154873.

17   Extract of poem 'no one died wishing', reproduced here with permission of the author Steven Shorrock. See https:// ptsdays.home.blog/2018/10/29/no-one-ever-died-wishing/

18   'Steve Jobs, 1955–2011'. Edited extract from Steve Job's commencement address to students graduating from Stanford University in 2005. The *Independent*, 7 October 2011, 11.

2. Accept Yourself

1   As a side note, the term 'unconditional self-regard' can seem a bit clumsy, but while it is similar to more popular terms like 'self-esteem', it is not the same. The idea of self-esteem by itself can be seen as promoting a form of selfishness and self-importance. People's self-esteem is often gained through doing better than others, being seen to perform well in the eyes of others or getting approval from people who are seen as more important. Unconditional self-regard is very much the opposite; how do we get to value ourselves in a way that isn't because we have beaten someone else in some race, or had applause or been given a gold star? For that reason, despite what might seem like a clumsier term, I felt it preferable to stick with it, so I hope you will bear with me, and appreciate the clarity of understanding that it brings.

2 Lepper, M. R., Greene, D. & Nisbett, R. E. (1973). 'Undermining Children's Intrinsic Interest with Extrinsic Reward: A Test of the "Overjustification." Hypothesis'. *Journal of Personality and Social Psychology*, *28*(1), 129–37. Deci, E. L., Koestner, R. & Ryan, R.M. (1999). 'A Meta-Analytic Review of Experiments Examining the Effects of Extrinsic Rewards on Intrinsic Motivation'. *Psychological Bulletin*. *125*(6), 627–68.

3 Davidai, S. & Gilovich, T. (2018). 'The Ideal Road Not Taken: The Self-Discrepancies Involved in People's Most Enduring Regrets'. *Emotion, 18*, 439–52.

4 Public Health England estimates that one in ten children suffer from a clinically significant mental health condition. See https://assets.publishing.service.gov.uk/government/uploads/system/uploads/attachment_data/file/575632/Mental_health_of_children_in_England.pdf

Also of interest: in a national US Survey of Children's Health, data from 2003, 2007 and 2011–12 was analyzed to estimate the prevalence of anxiety or depression among children aged six to seventeen years. Estimates were based on the parent report of being told by a healthcare provider that their child had the specified condition. By parent report, more than one in twenty children had current anxiety or depression in 2011–12. See, Bitsko, R. H., Holbrook, J. R., Ghandour, R. M., Blumberg, S. J., Visser, S. N., Perou, R. & Walkup, J. T. (2018). 'Epidemiology and Impact of Health Care Provider–Diagnosed Anxiety and Depression among US Children'. *Journal of Developmental and Behavioral Pediatrics, 39*(5), 395.

5   See for example, Brito, R., Joseph, S., & Sellman, E. (2022). From Instrumental to Integral Mindfulness: Toward a More Holistic and Transformative Approach in Schools. *Studies in Philosophy and Education*, 41(1), 91-109.

6   Statements are from the Unconditional Positive Self-Regard Scale developed by Tom Patterson and Stephen Joseph. See Patterson T. G. & Joseph, S. (2006). 'Development of a Self-report Measure of Unconditional Positive Self-regard'. *Psychology and Psychotherapy: Theory, Research and Practice*, 79(4), 557-70. And also, Patterson, T. G., & Joseph, S. (2013). 'Unconditional Positive Self-regard'. In Michael E. Bernard (ed.), *The Strength of Self-Acceptance: Theory, Practice and Research* (93–106). New York: Springer.

7   See, for example, Griffiths, L. J. & Griffiths, C. A. (2013). 'Unconditional Positive Self-Regard (UPSR) and Self-compassion, the Internal Consistency and Convergent/Divergent Validity of Patterson & Joseph's UPSR Scale'. *Open Journal of Medical Psychology*, 2(4), 168–74. doi: 10.4236/ojmp.2013.24026. Also, Murphy, D., Joseph, S., Demetriou, E. & Karimi-Mofrad, P. (2020). 'Unconditional Positive Self-Regard, Intrinsic Aspirations and Authenticity: Pathways to Psychological Well-Being'. *Journal of Humanistic Psychology*, 60(2), 258–79.

8   Neighbors, C., Larimer, M. E., Markman Geisner, I. & Knee, C. R. (2004). 'Feeling Controlled and Drinking Motives among College Students: Contingent Self-Esteem as a Mediator'. *Self and Identity*, 3(3), 207-24.

9   Chamberlain, J. M. & Haaga, D. A. (2001). 'Unconditional Self-Acceptance and Responses to Negative Feedback'. *Journal of Rational-Emotive and Cognitive-Behavior Therapy, 19*(3), 177–89.

3. Power Brokers

1   This term was used by Carl Rogers, for example: Rogers, C. R. (1959). 'A Theory of Therapy, Personality and Interpersonal Relationships, as Developed in the Client-Centred Framework'. In S. Koch (ed.) *Psychology: A Study of a Science, Vol. 3: Formulation of the Person and the Social Context* (184–256). New York: McGraw Hill.

2   Julian B. Rotter (1916–2014). Rotter, J. B. (1966). 'Generalized Expectancies for Internal Versus External Control of Reinforcement'. *Psychological Monographs: General and Applied, 80*(1), 1–27.

3   Levenson, H. (1974). 'Activism and Powerful Others: Distinctions within the Concept of Internal–External Control'. *Journal of Personality Assessment, 38*(4), 377–83.

4   Wallston, K. A., Strudler Wallston, B. & DeVellis, R. (1978). 'Development of the Multidimensional Health Locus of Control (MHLC) Scales'. *Health Education Monographs, 6*(1), 160–70.

5   Wallston, K. A., Malcarne, V. L., Flores, L., Hansdottir, I., Smith, C. A., Stein, M. J. & Clements, P. J. (1999). 'Does God Determine Your Health? The God Locus of Health Control Scale'. *Cognitive Therapy and Research, 23*(2), 131–42.

6   For example, see Fiori, K. L., Brown, E. E., Cortina,

K. S. & Antonucci, T. C. (2006). 'Locus of Control as a Mediator of the Relationship Between Religiosity and Life Satisfaction: Age, Race and Gender Differences'. *Mental Health, Religion and Culture, 9*(3), 239–63.

7 Albert Bandura (1925–2021). See Bandura, A. (1977). 'Self-efficacy: Toward a Unifying Theory of Behavioral Change'. *Psychological Review, 84*(2), 191–215. Also Bandura, A. (1986). *Social Foundations of Thought and Action: A Social Cognitive Theory.* Englewood Cliffs, NJ: Prentice-Hall.

8 Seeman, M. & Lewis, S. (1995). 'Powerlessness, Health and Mortality: A Longitudinal Study of Older Men and Mature Women'. *Social Science & Medicine, 41*(4), 517–25.

9 See Veenhoven, R. (2015). 'Happiness as a Priority in Public Policy'. In S. Joseph (ed.), *Positive Psychology in Practice: Promoting Human Flourishing in Work, Health, Education, and Everyday Life*, 731–50. Hoboken: Wiley.

10 Neal, A. G. & Seeman, M. (1964). 'Organizations and Powerlessness: A Test of the Mediation Hypothesis'. *American Sociological Review, 29*(2), 216–226.

11 Lee, E. H. & Schnall, S. (2014). 'The Influence of Social Power on Weight Perception'. *Journal of Experimental Psychology: General, 143*(4), 1719.

12 Galinsky, A. D., Gruenfeld, D. H. & Magee, J. C. (2003). 'From Power to Action'. *Journal of Personality and Social Psychology, 85*(3), 453–66.

13 See Myers, D. G., & Smith, S. M. (2012). *Exploring Social Psychology.* New York: McGraw-Hill, for a summary of these famous social psychology experiments. See also

Burger, J. M. (2009). 'Replicating Milgram: Would People Still Obey Today?' *American Psychologist, 64*(1), 1–11.

14   'English Landowners Have Stolen Our Rights', George Monbiot, *Guardian*, 19 August 2020. See https://www.theguardian.com/commentisfree/2020/aug/19/pandemic-right-to-roam-england

15   Twenge, J. M., Zhang, L. & Im, C. (2004). 'It's Beyond My Control: A Cross-Temporal Meta-Analysis of Increasing Externality in Locus Of Control, 1960–2002'. *Personality and Social Psychology Review, 8*(3), 308–19.

16   Friend, R., Rafferty, Y. & Bramel, D. (1990). 'A Puzzling Misinterpretation of the Asch "conformity study".' *European Journal of Social Psychology, 20*(1), 29–44. Twenge, J. M. (2009). 'Change Over Time in Obedience: The Jury's Still Out, But it Might Be Decreasing'. *American Psychologist, 64*(1), 28–31.

17   'Obituary of Lucille Times, Woman who inspired the Montgomery Bus Boycott'. *Irish Times*, 28 August 2012.

18   Evans, G. (1993). 'Class, Powerlessness and Political Polarization'. *European Journal of Social Psychology, 23*(5), 495–511.

19   Rainsford, E. (2017). 'Exploring Youth Political Activism in the United Kingdom: What Makes Young People Politically Active in Different Organisations?' *The British Journal of Politics and International Relations, 19*(4), 790–806.

20   Kifer, Y., Heller, D., Perunovic, W. Q. E. & Galinsky, A. D. (2013). 'The Good Life of the Powerful: The Experience of Power and Authenticity Enhances Subjective Well-Being'. *Psychological Science, 24*(3), 280–288.

4. Open Minded

1 Said by Roquentin, the protagonist of Jean-Paul Sartre's novel *Nausea*, trans. Lloyd Alexander (New York: New Directions, 1964, 39). First published in French in 1938.

2 Piaget, J. (1954). *The Construction of Reality in the Child*. New York: Basic Books.

3 Lerner, M. J. (1980). *The Belief in a Just World: A Fundamental Delusion*. New York: Plenum. See also, Furnham, A. (2003). 'Belief in a Just World: Research Progress over the Past Decade'. *Personality and Individual Differences, 34*(5), 795–817.

4 Andrews, G., Singh, M. & Bond, M. (1993). 'The Defense Style Questionnaire'. *Journal of Nervous and Mental Disease, 181*(4), 246–56.

5 Lee, S. (2020). *Be Water, My Friend: The True Teachings of Bruce Lee*. London: Rider, 76.

6 Joseph, S., Williams, R., Irwing, P. & Cammock, T. (1994). 'The Preliminary Development of a Measure to Assess Attitudes towards Emotional Expression'. *Personality and Individual Differences, 16*(6), 869–75.

7 Attitudes are associated with openness to experience, see Laghai, A. & Joseph, S. (2000). 'Attitudes Towards Emotional Expression: Factor Structure, Convergent Validity and Associations with Personality'. *British Journal of Medical Psychology, 73*(3), 381–84. Related to greater distress and lower social support, see Castle, H., Slade, P., Barranco-Wadlow, M. & Rogers, M. (2008). 'Attitudes to Emotional Expression, Social Support and Postnatal

Adjustment in New Parents'. *Journal of Reproductive and Infant Psychology*, *26*(3), 180-94. Associations with problems in living, including posttraumatic stress and eating distress, see Nightingale, J. & Williams, R. M. (2000). 'Attitudes to Emotional Expression and Personality in Predicting Post-traumatic Stress Disorder'. *British Journal of Clinical Psychology*, *39*(3), 243-54. Meyer, C., Leung, N., Barry, L. & De Feo, D. (2010). 'Emotion and Eating Psychopathology: Links with Attitudes Toward Emotional Expression Among Young Women'. *International Journal of Eating Disorders*, *43*(2), 187-89.

5. Becoming Lives

1   Frankl, V. (1959). *Man's Search for Meaning*. New York: Washington Square Press.

2   Huxley, A. (1998). *Brave New World* (1932). London: Vintage.

3   See for example Nafstad, H. (2015). 'Historical, Philosophical, and Epistemological Perspectives'. In S. Joseph (ed.), *Positive Psychology in Practice: Promoting Human Flourishing in Work, Health, Education and Everyday Life*. Hoboken: Wiley, 9-29.

4   Kasser, T. (2015). 'The Science of Values in the Culture of Consumption' In S. Joseph (ed.), *Positive Psychology in Practice: Promoting Human Flourishing in Work, Health, Education and Everyday Life*, 83-102. Hoboken: Wiley

5   Maslow, A. H. (1943). 'A theory of Human Motivation'. *Psychological Review*, *50*(4), 370.

6   The idea that materialism is connected to our

anxieties about death is supported by research: see Kasser, T. & Sheldon, K. M. (2000). 'Of Wealth and Death: Materialism, Mortality Salience, and Consumption Behavior'. *Psychological Science, 11*(4), 348–51.

7   Rogers, C. R. (1961). *On Becoming a Person*. Boston, MA: Houghton Mifflin.

8   In describing what the good life is, '... adjectives which seem more generally fitting are adjectives such as enriching, exciting, rewarding, challenging, meaningful.' Quoted in Rogers, C. R. (1963). 'The Concept of the Fully Functioning Person'. *Psychotherapy: Theory, Research & Practice, 1*(1), 17–26.

9   Oishi, S., Choi, H., Buttrick, N., Heintzelman, S. J., Kushlev, K., Westgate, E. C., ... & Besser, L. L. (2019). 'The Psychologically Rich Life Questionnaire'. *Journal of Research in Personality, 81*, 257–70.

10 Ottiger, A. S. & Joseph, S. (2021). 'From Ego-Centred to Eco-Centred: An Investigation of the Association between Authenticity and Ecological Sensitivity'. *Person-Centered & Experiential Psychotherapies, 20*(2), 139–51.

11 Kempton, B. (2018). *Wabi Sabi: Japanese Wisdom for a Perfectly Imperfect Life*. London: Piatkus.

12 Carnegie, D. (1948). *How To Stop Worrying and Start Living*. New York: Simon & Schuster.

6. Not Just You

1   'P is for Christopher Peterson. His Work on Positive Psychology'. *The Positive Encourager*. 'What makes life worth living?' (Part 1). https://www.thepositiveencourager.

global/christopher-petersons-work-on-positive-psychology-with-videos/

2 'Very Nice Guy (And Important Psychologist) Dies'. Robert Wright, *The Atlantic*, 14 October 2012.

3 Jonas, E., Schimel, J., Greenberg, J. & Pyszczynski, T. (2002). 'The Scrooge Effect: Evidence that Mortality Salience Increases Prosocial Attitudes and Behavior'. *Personality and Social Psychology Bulletin*, *28*(10), 1342–53.

4 'Lessons in the Good Life from Ground Hog Day', That Nerdy Catholic, 9 July 2021. https://www.youtube.com/watch?v=cxb4IMFUdy4

5 See Berger, E. M. (1952). 'The Relation between Expressed Acceptance of Self and Expressed Acceptance of Others'. *The Journal of Abnormal and Social Psychology*, *47*(4), 778-782. Omwake, K. T. (1954). 'The Relation between Acceptance of Self and Acceptance of Others Shown by Three Personality Inventories'. *Journal of Consulting Psychology*, *18*(6), 443.

6 Adler, A. (1921). *The Neurotic Constitution*. New York: Moffat, Yard.

7 Fromm, E. (1939). 'Selfishness and Self-love'. *Psychiatry*, *2*, 507–23.

8 Adapted from Pommier, E. A. (2011). 'The Compassion Scale. Dissertation Abstracts International Section A'. *Humanities and Social Sciences*, *72*, 1174.

9 See Bayır-Toper, A., Sellman, E. & Joseph, S. (2020). 'Being Yourself for the "Greater Good": An Empirical Investigation of the Moderation Effect of Authenticity

between Self-Compassion and Compassion for Others'. *Current Psychology*, 1–14. https://doi.org/10.1007/s12144-020-00989-6

10 Neff, K. D., Kirkpatrick, K. L. & Rude, S. S. (2007). 'Self-Compassion and Adaptive Psychological Functioning'. *Journal of Research in Personality*, *41*(1), 139–54.

11 Clifford, S. (2020). 'Compassionate Democrats and Tough Republicans: How ideology Shapes Partisan Stereotypes'. *Political Behavior*, *42*(4), 1269–93. Morris, S. G. (2020). 'Empathy and the Liberal–Conservative Political Divide in the US'. *Journal of Social and Political Psychology*, *8*(1), 8-24.

12 Emmons, R. A. & McCullough, M. E. (2003). 'Counting Blessings versus Burdens: An Experimental Investigation of Gratitude and Subjective Well-Being In Daily Life'. *Journal of Personality and Positive Psychology*, *84*, 377-389. https://doi.org/10.1037/0022-3514.84.2.377

13 Corbett, S. (2017). *How To Be a Craftivist*. London: Unbound.

14 Corbett, S. (Nov/Dec 2017). 'Changing the World One Stitch at a Time'. *Resurgence & Ecologist*, 305.

15 For a review of the evidence for the social conditions of happiness, see Veenhoven, R. (2015). 'Happiness as a Priority in Public Policy'. In S. Joseph (ed.), *Positive Psychology in Practice: Promoting Human Flourishing in Work, Health, Education, and Everyday Life*, 731–50. Hoboken: Wiley.

16 'Remarks by the President at a Memorial Service for the Victims of the Shooting in Tucson, Arizona'. 12

January 2011. https://obamawhitehouse.archives.gov/the-press-office/2011/01/12/remarks-president-barack-obama-memorial-service-victims-shooting-tucson